MAINE'S
HAIL TO THE CHIEF

MAINE'S HAIL TO THE CHIEF

A History of Presidential Visits to the Pine Tree State

MAC SMITH

Down East Books

Camden, Maine

Down East Books

An imprint of Globe Pequot
Trade division of The Rowman & Littlefield Publishing Group, Inc.
4501 Forbes Blvd., Ste. 200
Lanham, MD 20706
www.rowman.com

Distributed by NATIONAL BOOK NETWORK

Library of Congress Cataloging-in-Publication Data
Names: Smith, Mac, 1964- author.
Title: Maine's Hail to the Chief : a history of presidential visits to the
    Pine Tree State / Mac Smith.
Description: Lanham : Down East Books, [2021] | Includes bibliographical
    references.
Identifiers: LCCN 2021025258 (print) | LCCN 2021025259 (ebook) | ISBN
    9781684750122 (paperback) | ISBN 9781684750139 (ebook)
Subjects: LCSH: Presidents--United States--History. |
    Presidents--Travel--Maine. | Presidents--United States--Biography. |
    Maine--Politics and government--Miscellanea.
Classification: LCC E176.1 .S654 2021 (print) | LCC E176.1 (ebook) | DDC
    973.09/9--dc23
LC record available at https://lccn.loc.gov/2021025258
LC ebook record available at https://lccn.loc.gov/2021025259

Dedicated to Linsey, Mikey, and John, and their mother, Karen.

Contents

Introduction

Avisit from the president of the United States always brings excitement. In Maine, part of that excitement comes, perhaps, from the fact that we rarely see a president—only eighteen of the forty-five United States presidents have visited our state in our country's 244-year history.

The presidents that did visit Maine were reflective of the times in which they served. Many of the visits came at significant points in a presidency. Some visits had controversy, conflict, and ironic twists. For example, consider the following:

- During George Washington's visit, Maine was not even Maine, it was part of Massachusetts.
- President Ulysses S. Grant was the hero of the recently ended Civil War.
- President Benjamin Harrison's visit left many Bar Harbor people with a bad taste in their mouth.
- President Franklin Delano Roosevelt visited the state after a secret international meeting just before the United States joined World War II.
- President John F. Kennedy visited less than a month before his assassination.
- President Lyndon Baines Johnson visited, but it was the Secret Service that received most of the attention.
- President Richard Nixon was met with protests that saw Mainer battle Mainer.
- President Carter spent the night of his visit with a common, ordinary Maine family, in their modest home.

- President Trump's visit came in the middle of a global pandemic.

Besides visiting the cities of Maine, several presidents made their way to Bar Harbor for a brief rest. With its annual summer register of prominent national and international guests, Mount Desert Island was a safe place for a president to visit—you would have thought.

Another common thread of these visits is the importance played by Maine's James Blaine, a politician and statesman, and nearly the president of the United States. Blaine's Augusta home, where many of the presidents were entertained, is now Maine's official governor's residence, Blaine House.

All the Maine presidential visits left us with great stories, as well as a detailed view of Maine's lively history.

This is a look at the many times Maine has hailed to the chief.

George Washington

. . . barely set foot . . .

—Bangor Daily News

The first documented visit on Maine soil by a United States president was George Washington. In 1789 our nation's first chief executive made a trip to all thirteen states, a major undertaking in a pre-mechanized era.

According to the *Bangor Daily News* many years later, as part of this trip President Washington "barely set foot" in Kittery, Maine, at a time when Maine was part of Massachusetts.

James K. Polk

You don't know what a relief it is to be allowed to do exactly as I please once in a while.

—President James K. Polk

The second presidential visit to Maine came fifty-eight years after President Washington's, when James Knox Polk, the eleventh president of the United States, visited Maine's bigger cities.

Maine had only been a state for twenty-nine years when President Polk visited. He was fifty-one years old at the time and two years into his first term in office.

Born in a log cabin in Pineville, North Carolina, to a farmer, James K. Polk was a frail child. He would die less than two years after his visit to Maine, at the age of fifty-three. Polk was said to look exhausted when he left office at the end of his term, three months before his death.

Polk married Sarah Childress, a well-educated woman who assisted with her husband's political campaigns as well as his presidency.

During Polk's time in office, the only staff in the White House was Polk's own slaves. The Polk family continued to hold the slaves until the passage of the Thirteenth Amendment abolishing slavery sixteen years later.

In the summer of 1847 President Polk was traveling through New England, starting in New York and traveling through to Boston, and Lowell and Concord, New Hampshire. He was to visit Augusta on July 2 and go back through Portland the following day.

Upon hearing the news of Polk's visit, Bangor quickly arranged a presidential reception committee and on June 28, 1847, issued its own invitation to the White House:

To the Hon. James K. Polk, President of the United States

Sir:

At a meeting of the Mayor and Aldermen and Common Council of the City of Bangor, held this day, the following Order was unanimously passed in both branches:

. . . The undersigned members of the Committee would assure the President that the Order expresses the general wish of the inhabitants of this city to extend to him a cordial welcome on his arrival to this section of the country, and to promote the object of his tour, and contribute to his enjoyment in it. It is with pleasure, therefore, that they have been made the medium of this communication; and they would personally for themselves, and in behalf of the City Council, urge on the President, if consistent with the arrangements of his journey, to extend his visit to Bangor, and partake of the hospitalities so cordially tendered by the Order, and which, we assure him, will be highly agreeable to the citizens generally of the Eastern section of the State, and especially so to those of Bangor; and they request of him an answer at his earliest convenience.

With sentiments of high respect and consideration, we are your fellow citizens—

    Chas. Hayward

    John McDonald

    John S. Sayward

    S. P. Strickland

    S. Clinton Hatch

    J. E. Godfrey

Polk's reply came from Edmund Burke, the president's Commissioner of Patents:

Gentlemen:

I am requested by the President to inform you that he has received your letter on the 28th alt. communicating to him the Order of the City Authorities of Bangor, inviting him to visit that city during his present tour in the New England States. In reply he desires me to say, that his present engagements, and his determination to return to Washington as soon as circumstances will permit, compel him very reluctantly to decline the invitation to visit the city of Bangor, so kindly and courteously tendered through you, as the organs and the authorities and people of your city.

The firing of a cannon at Mt. Joy and the ringing of the city bells announced the arrival of President Polk in Portland on Friday, July 2, 1847 at noon.

Polk's train was received by the Portland Mayor Eliphalet Greeley, members of the Portland City Council, and the event's Committee of Arrangements.

"The weather was exceedingly fine; and the views of the city, the distant bay and islands, the ocean beyond Cape Elizabeth, and particularly the unfinished breakwater, must have been highly gratifying to the President" wrote the *Portland Advertiser*.

The crowd was dense in the immediate vicinity of President Polk's arrival. His welcome and remarks lasted about a half an hour, and then Polk and his party entered a carriage procession that consisted of approximately thirty carriages. The presidential procession was accompanied by the Young Men's Cavalcade, the Portland Light Infantry, and a portion of the Portland Fire Department, in total about four hundred men. About two hundred students from the Portland public schools lined the procession route along State Street, some with wreaths in their hands. A few times the crowd attempted a group cheer, but it was never successful.

"Very few people, apparently, were in from the country, occupied with what one might have reasonably expected, and altogether the throng in the streets was not by any means so great as we anticipated," wrote the *Advertiser.*

As the procession reached the Eastern Promenade, a group of railroad workers let off half a score of explosive charges.

"An appropriate tribute of repeat to one so heartedly favorable to internal improvements—as well as an excellent application of gunpowder," wrote the *Advertiser.*

The plan had been for the president to personally meet the people assembled in front of the Portland Exchange, the building in Portland that held most federal offices, but due to the large turnout at the exchange, the plans quickly changed. Instead, Polk was escorted directly into the exchange building, to the personal rooms of the mayor. Polk was then escorted to the second-floor balcony of the exchange, a more practical place from which to address the larger-than-expected crowd.

From the balcony, Mayor Greeley introduced President Polk to the citizens below.

President Polk complimented the citizens of Portland and the city itself, and said he wished he could stay longer but that he had other engagements. The president's brief speech was met with a legitimate, hearty cheer, "the only one we heard during the day," said the *Advertiser.*

A veteran who was severely wounded at the battle of Buena Vista was also introduced to the crowd and received the same cheer.

At 4:00 p.m. the president and his party had dinner at the U.S. Hotel in Portland. Reporters were not invited. The evening in Portland ended with fireworks at Portland City Hall, entertaining a vast crowd that had assembled at sunset and stayed after the fireworks ended.

Leaving that night from Portland, President Polk made his way to Hallowell aboard the steam ship *Huntress.*

It was late at night, and the *Huntress* was running late. The assembled crowd at the Hallowell boat landing watched in the growing darkness of the summer's night for light from the presidential ship.

At midnight, the *Huntress* hove into view. On the first sight of the ship, cannons were fired by the gunners who were standing by.

"The first glimmer of light and the first faint chug of her paddles set the bells a-ringing in Hallowell, and the bell-ringers at Augusta heard the sound and joined the chorus," wrote the *Advertiser.*

A display of fireworks caused a bright illumination of the city. Polk arrived in Augusta in "a style of great splendor," said the *Bangor Whig and Courier*, whose editor had been on the committee to invite Polk to Bangor.

President Polk and his entourage were met by the Portland Reception Committee, R. D. Rice, G. W. Stanley, W. A Drew, E. Bronson, G. White, J. H. Williams, and J. A. Petteingild, and escorted to awaiting carriages.

From the steamer landing in Hallowell to the east side of the Kennebec River in Augusta, all along the carriage procession route people rushed to the windows and freshened the candles that were burning to show a welcome to the president.

"The housewives who had frugally waited for the President's coming before starting the illumination now lit up their windows for the first time, and history records that from Hallowell to Augusta, along the line of travel there was hardly a house which had not its welcoming lights," said the *Lewiston Evening Journal*.

As the presidential procession made its way to the State House in Augusta, they saw that every window in the building held candles. A score of willing youngsters had been recruited to light the numerous candles at a prearranged signal and to stand by them to make sure none went out as the procession proceeded along. Every hotel window along State Street was lit with candles.

The procession crossed the bridge and stopped at the mansion of former Maine Senator Reuel Williams, situated high on the hill above old Fort Western. The spot had a rich view of the Kennebec Valley. Senator Williams, noted for his hospitality, welcomed his guests, President Polk and Secretary of State James Buchanan, on the house's portico. The men were ushered into the spacious parlors, decorated with mahogany and brass, the walls beautifully adorned. Polk and Buchanan stayed the night there, while others in the party were entertained at the home of Daniel Williams on Myrtle Street.

The next morning, despite the numerous offerings of his host, President Polk simply ate milk and bread for breakfast, telling Mrs. Williams that it was the best thing he had eaten since he left the White House.

"You don't know what a relief it is to be allowed to do exactly as I please once in a while," the president told Mrs. Williams. "There has been so much of eating and dining all the way down to your beautiful state that it is almost more than the mortal frame can stand."

Polk's "black servant" told a reporter that there was never such good cooking as that of Maine.

While Polk was eating his bread and milk, the front yard of the Williams mansion was slowly filling with citizens anxious to get a peek at the president, maybe even a handshake. Hundreds of citizens would ultimately gather there, and hundreds more would line the streets leading to the Williams mansion.

Inside the house, Mr. Williams suggested that President Polk show himself at the front door and at least bow his acknowledgements. The crowd cheered wildly when Polk emerged on the portico, standing and smiling. Seeing that the president was somewhat uncomfortable, Mrs. Williams joined her guest.

"Mr. President, you are making a great many of your people very, very happy," Mrs. Williams said to Polk as they stood together on the portico.

"Madam, they are my masters, I am their servant," Polk replied with a bow.

The people nearest the house heard the words and passed them to the people behind them, and as the president's words spread, the crowed began a cheer of graciousness. President Polk bowed to the crowd again and returned to the inside of the house. He then held an informal reception in the parlor of the house for a few invited guests.

General A. Redington, Marshal of the Day, arrived at the Williams home and told President Polk that his escort to the State House was ready and the procession to the Augusta State House would begin as soon as the president said so.

In an open barouche, President Polk bowed his thanks to the now thousands of people who lined the streets near the Williams mansion. Men stood with bared heads along the entire line of the procession and cheered lustily as the executive carriage passed.

At the state house, President Polk was escorted to the Hall of Representatives to address the Maine legislature, which was gathered in joint convention. Governor John W. Dana of Fryeburg welcomed the president:

Permit me, as the organ of the constituted authorities of Maine, to tender to you, in their behalf, her courtesies and hospitalities," said Governor Dana.

We tender them to you as the Chief Magistrate of a Republic whose youthful energy and progress give sure promise, that, in her approaching maturity, she must exert a controlling influence over the destinies of the world.

We beg you, too, as the representative of the whole Union, comprising institutions in many respects dissimilar, to regard our cordial welcome as an evidence that Maine in her sympathies knows no geographical limit—that she never will permit their patriotic attachment to every member of the Confederacy to be weakened by appeals to local prejudices or sectional jealousies.

In judging of the capabilities of our State, we would with pride direct your attention to our commercial, our navigating, our fishing, our lumbering, our mineral, our agricultural, and our manufacturing resources, and ask you to count, if you can, their value and importance or fix upon the date of their exhaustion.

Permit me again, on behalf of our citizens, to bid you a most hearty, cordial welcome to the state.

President Polk gave his reply:

Mr. Governor: It is seldom the good fortune of any man to be the recipient of such distinguished consideration as that bestowed on me today, by the highest constituted authorities of the state. I can however, in no sense appropriate to myself personally the homage which has marked my reception here. I receive it, therefore, as an homage rendered to the institutions of the country, in the person of its chief magistrate, who is but the servant of the people, charged, for the time being, with the administration of the government.

President Polk went on to thank God for our sovereign nation. He spoke of the need to protect that sovereignty and the style of government designed by the founding fathers, "With our obligation to do so,

I have been most sensibly impressed by my visit to the people of your State, who, while they so extremely enjoy its privileges and its blessings, cannot fail to appreciate its value."

Polk said that Maine's style of government was achieved by compromise and spoke of the usefulness of that compromise. He spoke of the need to preserve the Union.

> It is but fifty-eight years since the formation of this confederacy, and when, fifty-eight years hence, a president of the United States, one, perchance, not now in existence, shall visit you and be the welcomed and honored guest of the executive and authorities of Maine, who shall estimate the vastness of this already great country?
>
> Sir, I am informed that this is the first time that a chief magistrate of the republic has ever visited your state, it is also the first time that I have had the pleasure to come among this portion of my fellow citizens. I recognize in them all my brethren and rejoice in the further fact that while we can sink all considerations that do not harmonize with the whole good of the different sections of our common country, we afford an asylum for the oppressed of other lands. Those who gave us our form of government bade the emigrant welcome to our shores—invited him to come and partake of the bounties spread before us, and gave him the assurance that he had only to act the part of an honest man to be entitled to protection in all his rights.

At the conclusion of the president's speech, the two houses of the Maine State Legislature adjourned, and President Polk was escorted to the front steps of the State House, where he addressed the immense awaiting crowd. The presidential party then was driven to the Augusta House, where an elaborate state banquet was served. It was said that $700 worth of rum was consumed during the banquet.

"This of itself gives some idea of the crowd that must have gathered—for rum in those days was not an expensive tipple," said the *Lewiston Evening Journal* in 1902.

Also at the banquet were Maine's United States senators James W. Bradbury of Augusta and George Evans of Gardiner, and many prominent state officials, including former Maine Governor John Fairfield of Saco, Robert Dunlap of Brunswick, Hugh J. Anderson of Belfast, Governor John Hubbard of New Hampshire, Governor Alexandre Moulton of Louisiana, United States Navy Commodore Charles Stewart, Attorney General of the United States, and Commissioner of Patents Edmund Burke,

At the conclusion of the banquet the presidential party was driven across the Kennebec River to Gardiner. President Polk made a brief response in the presence of one of the largest crowds ever seen by that city.

The president spent the night at the Oaklands as the guest of Robert Hallowell Gardiner, a member of the family for whom the city was named.

On Sunday morning President Polk went to religious services at two different churches. He visited the Hon. Asa Clapp, and in the evening had tea at the home of former Maine Senator John Anderson.

On Monday evening the mayor and members of the Augusta City Council called upon the president at Mrs. Jones's boarding house, where President Polk had spent part of his visit. They stayed for a visit and then accompanied the president to the special train on which President James K. Polk left the state at about 7:30 p.m.

3

Ulysses S. Grant

The close observer would look in vain in his appearance for the evidences of that Caesarism with which one of the leading dailies of New York is charging him in its columns. There is nothing to distinguish his appearance from that of any private citizen.

—*Bangor Whig and Courier*

President Ulysses S. Grant was a United States hero, at least in the Northern states. In 1864 President Abraham Lincoln promoted Grant to the rank of Lieutenant General, a rank held only by George Washington. Grant's victories as a general in the Union Army during the Civil War not only helped preserve the fledgling union, but they helped cement him as a legend of his time.

Born in Point Pleasant, Ohio, Ulysses S. Grant graduated from West Point and served in the Mexican-American War. He married Julia Dent, and together the couple had four children.

On August 2, 1865, four years before being elected president, Grant would travel by train from Portland to Brunswick to attend the commencement exercises of Bowdoin College and to receive an honorary degree. At the ceremony, General Grant was joined by Bowdoin alumnus General Joshua Chamberlain, another Civil War hero, on the stage of the First Parish Congregational Church in Brunswick. This was just six years after the conclusion of the Civil War.

Grant was elected as the youngest president in the 19th century, in an Electoral College landslide. Grant was credited with stabilizing the post-war national economy, creating the Department of Justice, prosecuting the Ku Klux Klan, appointing African Americans and

Jews to prominent federal offices, and creating the first Civil Service Commission.

Two-and-a-half years after being elected President, Grant again paid a call to the state of Maine.

"Let us have everything in the shape of bunting flying in the breeze, in honor of our Chief Magistrate PRESIDENT GRANT, at sunrise on a Wednesday next, Oct. 18th," was a notice run in the *Bangor Whig & Courier* by the Bangor Presidential Reception Committee.

The committee requested that people living along the procession route decorate their houses with bunting, flags, mottoes, whatever they might have that was patriotic, the day before Grant's visit. The Illumination Committee requested that people living along the procession route illuminate their residences.

Calvin Kirk, Bangor's Harbor Master, urged all vessels, from the largest to the smallest, to set their colors, "whether torn or old."

Local shops were prepared to fill the community's needs in welcoming the president, and they advertised that fact in the local newspapers.

> How Shall We Decorate?
>> Everyone is Asking.
>> The Decorations that will please
>> General Grant
>> The best, will be to see a NEW PAIR OF BOOTS or a new
>> FALL STYLE HAT, from WOOD'S
>> Now we advise everyone who wants to have a good time, and
>> enjoy the coming celebration,
>> to go at once and select some
>> New Boots or Hat,
>> FROM THE
>> BEST STOCK EVER OFFERED IN BANGOR
>> We have just opened an elegant line of
>> Carriage Shawls
>> and
>> HORSE BLANKETS

a best-ever shown in the place, and as General Grant is a great
lover of a fine team you will not want to be seen with an old
faded Robe or blanket, so now will be the time to replenish.
Don't forget the place.
At WOOD'S
Corner of Main and Hammond St's.

Something to Eat!
Will be the cry during the President's visit, and parties wishing extra dishes should hand in their orders in season, or they
may be disappointed.
We cater for President Grant's Supper,
the 17th, and can fill a few more orders for
New Hams, Beef Tongues, Poultry and Game, Oysters
received daily at LOW'S MARKET.
No. 2 Kenduskeag Block

STONE & JONES
The Illumination. Messrs. Wood, Bishop and Co. have for
sale a large quantity
of those convenient little tin candle-sticks that can be easily
attached
to a window-sash for illuminating purposes.

New uniforms were given to the men of Bangor's No. 3 Fire Engine
Company in preparation of the president's visit. The uniform consisted
of a blue cloth shirt with a red shield on the breast, on which an eagle
was embroidered in gold. There were drab pants with a scarlet stripe,
blue caps of a navy pattern with patent-leather visor, over which was
embroidered in gold an eagle and the name and number of the fire
company. There were even new belts of black patent leather, trimmed
with white, the clasp a gilt-bronze, bearing the words "Eagle 3-Bangor."
"The uniform is one of the finest ever worn by a fire company, and
the 'Old Threes' will look positively gorgeous in it," said the *Bangor
Whig & Courier.*

The Jameson Guards of Bangor, a volunteer military infantry, had never had a flag. For some time, a lady in Bangor had started a subscription to obtain one for them. Unknown to the Guards, the flag was purchased in time for Grant's visit. The Guards were ordered to muster on Friday, four days before the president's visit, at 12:00 noon. At the Guards' assembly, a long, mysterious-looking box was presented. As the box was opened, someone cried out "It's a flag!"

A loud cheer burst forth at the news. The flag was a national ensign of silk, fringed with gold bullion, and mounted upon a hickory staff, terminating in a gold globe surmounted by an eagle in the same metal. A sliver plate on the staff had engraved upon it the following inscription: "Presented to the Jameson Guards by the Ladies of Bangor. October 1871."

The yard in front of the Maine Central Station was levelled and graveled for the better footing of the president's military escort.

The Committee on Hospitality used the Common Council Room at Bangor City Hall as their visit headquarters on Tuesday and Wednesday. They urged anyone in the city having spare rooms to place them at the disposal of the committee.

"Our hotels are already pledged to their utmost capacity, and unless the people respond liberally, many of our invited guests must receive very meagre attention," read a newspaper notice from the committee.

People who had already donated rooms were warned that trains might be delayed, and they should be prepared to greet visitors at a late hour.

The public was also warned against "Pickpockets and sneak thieves."

"We renew our warning that there will doubtless be a large number of pick-pockets and thieves in this city tomorrow, who will come here to ply their vocation in the immense crowd sure to be present. Look out for them, and besides, don't leave your houses without being sure that the windows and doors are fastened," said the *Bangor Whig and Courier.*

There had been some concern that President Grant would not arrive. One reporter told of an overheard conversation before the president's visit. A person who doubted Grant would arrive said so to a veteran.

"I've fought under Grant, Sir, and I always noticed that when he said he was going anywhere, he went," the veteran replied.

On Tuesday, October 17, 1871, President Grant and his party arrived in Maine. The voyage to Maine on the train was described as very pleasant in every respect, and rapidly made, despite a slight accident on the Presumpscot Bridge when the train collided with a cow. The president was accompanied on his trip by many cabinet members. His wife, Julia, had gone to New York.

The presidential train consisted of seven cars, two of which were given to the Capital Guards of Augusta. Two Pullman cars were devoted respectively to the President and the Governor General of Canada. The other three cars were used for members of the presidential party and the governor-general's party, and members of the press.

President Grant was coming to Bangor to attend ceremonies celebrating the opening of the North Atlantic Railway, which would join Maine and Canada. The railroad was built with government and state aid for the purpose of giving direct rail communication between the United States and the Canadian Maritime Provinces. It was expected that the railroad would greatly reduce the time of travel between New York and England and greatly facilitate mail communication between the two countries. The railroad cost $4.5 million dollars, almost $100 million in 2020 dollars.

"The railroad itself has proved a great factor in the upbuilding of Bangor and eastern Maine" said the *Bangor Whig and Courier.*

President Grant's train was met and joined in Portsmouth, New Hampshire, by most of Maine's Congressional Delegation: Congressman James Blaine, Congressman John Peters, and Senator Hannibal Hamlin.

James Gillespie Blaine of Augusta is a name that threads throughout the Maine presidential visits, and each presidential visit marks a change in Blaine's national political career.

Blaine was one of the 19th century's leading Republicans. As a young man he married Harriet Stanwood, a teacher and Maine native, while they were both teaching in Kentucky. The Blaines would return to Maine when the Kennebec Journal came up for sale and was purchased by Blaine. With the help of the financially successful newspaper, Blaine began a career in politics.

Hannibal Hamlin was a native of Paris, Maine. He was a newspaper editor who would go on to serve in Congress. Ultimately Hamlin would become the fifteenth vice president of the United States.

At Kittery, President Grant was informally welcomed by General J. A. Hall on behalf of Maine Governor Sidney Perham.

Grant's train arrived at Portland at noon and was received with a presidential salute of artillery. There was no ceremony and no speech, the decision already having been made to celebrate the president on his return through Portland at the end of his visit, when he would have more time.

John Young, Governor General of Canada, which was still part of Great Britain, joined the presidential party at Portland. The presidential train left at 12:30 p.m.

In Brunswick, Joshua Chamberlain, who had just completed his term as Maine's governor, introduced President Grant to the large, enthusiastic crowd when the president's train arrived at 1:25 p.m. Grant was at the train station for about twenty minutes.

In Maine's capitol, a huge crowd had turned out. Upon President Grant's 3 p.m. arrival in Augusta, bells started ringing and a salute was fired from the U.S. Arsenal. The city's public buildings and many private homes were richly decorated. Grant was formally welcomed to the state by Governor Perham. Augusta Mayor Joseph Eveleth introduced Grant to the vast crowd, who received their president with deafening cheers.

"It affords me great pleasure to welcome you to the State of Maine and its capitol," said Mayor Eveleth. "On behalf of our people I extend to you a hearty greeting and tender their most generous hospitality. Please accept the assurance of our high appreciation of your character as a citizen, and your distinguished services both as the commander of our victorious army, and as the chief executive of the nation. We earnestly hope your visit to Maine will be as pleasant to you as it is gratifying to us."

President Grant replied that he wished to thank the people of the state, through their governor, for the uniform courtesy and kindness that he had always received at their hands, and especially for the cordial welcome that he received here six years ago during his visit to Bowdoin

College, and for the very flattering manner in which he was received this day. Grant said the he had no doubt that his stay of a few days would be as pleasant to him as it could possibly be to others.

Grant remained on the platform to greet citizens for a half an hour. At 3:30 p.m. the presidential train departed the station and started the trip to Bangor amid the cheers of the assembled thousands, who filled every possible space in the vicinity of the Augusta depot.

In Bangor, the day of President Grant's visit was much like a holiday. Freight trains would not be run that day, and no freight was received or delivered, as ordered by L. L. Lincoln, Assistant Superintendent of the Maine Central Railroad.

People had been coming into the city all day. A special train ran between Old Town and Bangor in the evening so that neighboring towns could attend the torch-light presidential procession.

A calcium light was set opposite of the railroad depot, and in the evening it threw an intense light upon the front of the Maine Central Railroad building. Military companies were marched to the Maine Central Station at 6 p.m. in preparation of greeting and escorting the president.

After several small stops along the rail line to Bangor, the train carrying President Grant and his entourage arrived in Bangor at 6:35 p.m.

Immediately two twenty-one gun salutes were fired, one for the President of the United States, and one for the Governor-General of Canada.

President Grant was met in Bangor by various state and local officials, and a very large crowd. With the presidential party safely in their carriages, escorted by a military squad and flanked by 200 firemen from Bangor and Brewer, the procession moved through Summer Street to Union Street, up Union to High Street, through High to Hammond Street, down Hammond to Main Street, and up Main to the historic Bangor House, where President Grant and his party would stay for the night.

The crowd of people who came out to see the president of the United States in Bangor was dense and occupied every available inch of space on the streets through which Grant's procession passed. The houses, blocks and stores on the route were brilliantly illuminated and decorated with flags, bunting, lanterns, and transparencies. Long strings of Chinese lanterns hung a number of places across Main Street.

President Grant was met with enormous crowds, including many school children of Bangor waiting along the parade route on Broadway, ready to sing to Grant. The children sang their songs and presented bouquets of flowers.

"The music of the bands, the tramp of the troops, the cheers of the excited crowds, the flashing of the torches and the dazzling illumination all combined to form a scene such as was never before witnessed in Maine, and will never be forgotten by those fortunate enough to witness it," wrote the *Whig and Courier*.

After arriving at the Bangor House, Grant's first stop was the dining room in the northeast corner of the second floor, one floor below his private rooms for the visit. Canadian Governor General Young had apartments on the third floor, in the northwest corner of the building, and the rest of the presidential party also shared the same floor.

The governor general retired early that night, fatigued from his trip. President Grant, however, and others, including Speaker Blaine, took tea with Senator Hamlin at his residence on Fifth Street, where they were joined by a few other gentleman and ladies.

Because of the lateness of the hour of President Grant's arrival and the early hour of darkness at that time of year, most of the celebration of the president's arrival was saved for the following day, Wednesday, October 18.

On Wednesday morning the weather was bright and fair. The streets were alive at an early hour with people. Farmers from the surrounding communities were present in large numbers, selling produce and provisions to the large crowd of people who had descended upon Bangor, and the hotels and rooming houses where they lodged.

"There seemed to be plenty, notwithstanding the unusually great demand, and prices were very little above the average," wrote the *Whig and Courier*.

The Maine Central Railroad was decorated in red, white, and blue, with a shield, and English and American flags on the west entrance. On the north end of the station was an American eagle. Flags had been placed at every corner of the building.

Several state infantry groups participated in the Bangor festivities. As each group arrived at the train station by special train, they were met by the Committee on Military and the Jameson Guards, and escorted to their guest quarters. Arriving military units included the Portland Light Infantry, Portland Mechanic Blues, Auburn Light Infantry, Norway Light Infantry, Belfast City Guards, and the Skowhegan Light Infantry.

Bangor's neighboring towns also participated in the parade, including Orono, who sent one of their fire engines, the Monitor, and Bucksport, who sent a fire engine and the Bucksport Cornet Band. Music for the parade and festivities was also provided by the Bangor Cornet Band, Johnson's Cornet Band of Lewiston, the Norway Cornet Band of Norway, the Portland Band, the Thomaston Band, the Augusta Band, and the Lynn Cornet Band of Lynn, Massachusetts,

There were lumbermen in the parade, in uniform, from lumbermills owned by citizens of Bangor:

- 200 lumbermen from James Walker's mills at Basin Mills
- 150 lumbermen from Palmer & Johnson's mills at Brewer
- 150 lumbermen from William T. Pearson's mills at Great Works
- 150 lumbermen from Cutler, Thatcher & Co.'s mills at Bradley
- 75 lumbermen from Roberts & Co.'s mills at Old Town.

Presidential military escorts were ordered to form promptly on the corner of Harlow and State streets at 8 a.m., with some personnel reporting for duty at the Bangor House.

The route of the parade for President Grant was down Main Street, across the Kenduskeag Bridge, up State Street to French Street, up French to Somerset Street, through Somerset to Broadway, through Broadway to York Street, up York to Newbury Street, up Newbury to State Street, down State, and again across the Kenduskeag Bridge, up Hammond Street to Ohio Street, up Ohio to Hudson Street, through Hudson to Union Street, and then down Union to the Bangor House.

A horse standing in front of Wheelwright, Clark & Company, owned by the senior member of the firm, was frightened by the flags hung across the street and ran across the bridge, upsetting the vehicle to which he was attached and finally clearing himself from it by collision with a telegraph pole. This accident caused a change in the original parade route.

All business in Bangor was suspended in observance of President Grant's visit. All the public buildings in the city were decorated with mottoes, flags, bunting, and other patriotic decorations, under the direction of the Decorating Committee, who secured the services of Col. Beals and Sons of Boston. Ornamental arches were erected over several streets at prominent points.

The *Whig and Courier* listed private residents by street and described how each house had been decorated. For example:

- On Union Street one arch read "OUR PRESIDENT, PEACE WELCOMES YOU.
- At the head of Main Street was a beautiful arch, surmounted with American and British flags, and which read "Welcome to the Nation's Guest."
- Tasteful decorations heavily adorned the store fronts all along Main Street.
- Owen McCann's residence, large American banner, and flag of Erin.
- Chas. Hayward, tri-colored festoons, American flags, etc.

"To name the places decorated would be simply to name all the business houses on the street," wrote the *Whig and Courier.*

The Wheelwright and Clark's block was especially notable, every window in the large structure adorned by seven flags—American and British—while large ensigns were hung all over the lower story. The roof was bordered with hundreds of tiny flags.

Kenduskeag Bridge was decorated. Everything seemed to be decorated, including the Penobscot County Jail. The jail presented a beautiful front in tri-colored festoons, with shield, stand of colors and English ensigns over portico, winged out with large American flags. This was described as one of the most unique and tasteful decorations on the route.

"The motto 'Welcome' was appropriately conspicuous for its absence," wrote the *Whig and Courier.*

The carriages of President Grant and the rest of the presidential procession made their way through the streets of Bangor, thronged with thousands of citizens wanting to catch a glimpse of the Civil War hero and president of the United States.

At 1:00 p.m. Grant's carriage arrived in front of Norumbega Hall, immediately followed by the other distinguished officials. President Grant was met by Bangor Mayor Samuel Dale and members of the Committee of Arrangements, consisting of Isaac R. Clark, R. S. Morison, Eugene F. Sanger, G. W. Ladd, A. B. Farnham, Moses Giddings, James Tobin, J. G. Clark, John H. Rice, and H. H. Fogg.

Mayor Dale escorted the presidential party inside for the celebration of the opening of the North Atlantic Railroad. From 1:00 to 3:30 p.m., a Collation and Ceremonies was provided in Norumbega Hall for the guests of the city and for the members of the public who were able to buy one of the limited number of tickets to the event.

All week the organizing committee had been asking for people to donate any flowers to the Committee on Collation, and to drop them off at Norumbega Hall.

"A great many flowers will be needed to decorate the tables properly, and we hope the supply will equal the demand," wrote the committee in a newspaper notice.

Norumbega Hall presented what was called a gorgeous appearance both outside and in. Among the decorations, the front of the balcony was draped in white, with blue stars, below which there were festoons of red, white, and blue bunting. On the right of the balcony was an arch bearing the word "Grant" in gold letters on a blue ground; on the left, a similar arch with the words "Victoria," and in the center another having the word "Fraternity." In the rear of the balcony was a large ornamental piece, on which was inscribed the words "The day we celebrate."

The hall was lavishly decorated from one end to the other. The flags of all nations were hung from the ceiling, arranged by complimenting colors. The stage was carpeted with green, and the front of the stage was draped with pink. On the extreme front of the stage was a large gilt eagle. The rear of the stage was adorned by a larger-than-life portrait of President George Washington.

"The interior of the hall is very beautifully decorated, showing much skill on the part of Col. Beals & Sons," wrote the *Whig and Courier.*

On the walls of the gallery were the flags of the various military companies involved in the ceremonies.

The seats on the floor and in the galleries were soon filled, and shortly after the opening of the doors, some 700 people, including quite a large number of ladies, were in position for the duties and pleasures of the hour.

The collation was presided over by Mayor Dale and Sen. Hamlin.

Mayor Dale opened the ceremony by asking a minister to provide a divine blessing. Blessings were requested for the celebration, for the amicable relations between Maine and Canada, and for the banquet in which they were about to partake.

Food service then began, promptly and efficiently.

The tables in the hall were covered with spotless white tablecloths and elegantly adorned with fresh flowers by a Boston florist.

The menu included cold turkey, cold chicken, cold ham, cold tongue, potted pigeons, escalloped oysters and cranberry jelly. Relishes included Piccalilli and chow chow. Salads included chicken salad and lobster salad. Pastries included apple pie, lemon pie, custard pie, mince pie, squash pie and Washington pie. Desert included cakes—almond, lady, currant, sponge, and fruit. Fruit included oranges, apples, grapes, nuts, and raisins. Tea and coffee were also served at the conclusion of the meal. All offerings were in abundance.

Mayor Dale welcomed President Grant, Governor General Young of Canada, and the others in the presidential party after the meal. The mayor's remarks were short but eloquent and were often interrupted by applause. The assembled crowd toasted President Grant with hearty cheers.

The governor general of Canada thanked the crowd for its welcome on behalf of his sovereigns. Young said he had always heard the English were not welcome in the United States, especially New England. That statement was met with shouts of "No! No!" from the crowd. He went on to say that notion was dispelled after he arrived in Bangor and found the Union Jack floating amicably side by side with the starry flag of our country and elevated to honored positions by American hands, and he said he was convinced that the difference was not irreconcilable. His words and sentiment were met with cheers.

The Canadian governor general said he believed a friendly feeling had been ignited by the Treaty of 1871, which had been ratified just a few months previously and which settled differences between the United States and Great Britain arising from the Civil War and other matters.

The crowd stood and applauded. The Canadian governor was described as being visibly moved by the standing ovation. In celebration, "God Save The Queen" and "Yankee Doodle Dandy" were sung as a blended song.

At 4:30 p.m. the presidential party left the hall, "closing the most important gathering ever held in this city or in the State of Maine, with a cordiality of feeling that will pulsate Eastward and Westward to the utmost boundaries of the two English-speaking nations." wrote the Whig and Courier.

There then was a public reception at Norumbega Hall, no ticket required. Grant greeted many people, including Civil War veterans who broke through the lines to shake the hand of General Grant. The festivities went on so long that they eventually had to be stopped due to darkness.

There was a military review and bayonet drill in Davenport Square by the state military companies who were in attendance that day, in the presence of the presidential party. After the reception and military review, President Grant and his party were taken in carriages to the residence of Mayor Samuel H. Dale.

Wrote the *Whig and Courier*:

> At this late hour we are unable to convey as we would wish, our thanks to all the friends who have contributed to the success of our efforts, but we wish the military companies, the fire companies, the bands and others who leave us to-morrow, to bear with them our cordial thanks for the efficient cooperation they have afford, and to assure them all that Bangor will always have a hearty welcome for them. The street display has never been equaled in this State, and the man or woman who could look upon the soldiery bearing of the troops on yesterday and not feel proud of our Volunteer Militia, must at least be particularly constituted.

The unanimity and zeal with which our citizens have contributed in every way to the success of the programme, the beautifying of the City and the enjoyment of our guests, is beyond all praise, and will gain its best reward in the pleasant recollections of a day which will stand out brightly in the history of Bangor.

The celebration of the previous day also caught the attention of the national newspapers, including the *Boston Journal*:

The somewhat elaborate program devised to mark appropriately the formal opening of the European and North American Railway from Bangor, Me., to St. John, N.B. has been handsomely and most successfully carried out the past week. From the beginning to the end, even down to the minutest details, there was evidence of happy forethought and the presence of a master mind. And perhaps the highest and truest praise we can offer is to say that the ceremonies were conducted throughout in a style and spirit worthy of the grand occasion.

To the President and Directors of the European and North American Railway, and especially to the large-hearted, wide-awake people of Bangor, is great credit due. The latter not only decorated and illuminated their dwellings tastefully and lavishly in honor of the occasion, but they opened them for the accommodation of the large number of invited guests from abroad, who were made to feel at home. Indeed, the Bangoreans seemed to vie with each other in acts of hospitality, and to this fact quite as much as for its importance and the presence of distinguished men, will the occasion be remembered by the many strangers present . . . then the six hundred stalwart, red-shirted lumbermen presented a sight worth seeing, while it was refreshing to listen to their hearty, ringing cheers, as they passed by the President. . . . This was the only time we saw a smile flit over the immobile face of our President. He seemed affected by the novel spectacle.

There was an excursion on Thursday to Vanceboro to continue the ceremonies associated with the opening of the railroad. The trip was by invitation only, and official cards were necessary before entering the special train. Two trains of nine elegant new cars each left Front Street just above the steamboat wharves in Bangor for Vanceboro. President Grant and his party took the rear car of the first train.

On the ride back from Vanceboro, the *Bangor Whig and Courier* had a chance to talk to President Grant.

We found no evidence of taciturnity, but contrawise a lucency and felicity of expression surpassed by very few persons whom we have ever met. Our part in the conversation was principally confined to queries and brief responses, and President Grant gave his views on every subject presented with an unreserve and a terse, comprehensive style, as admirable as the soundness of his conclusions.

At every station, where the people had gathered in the darkness and sleet to catch a glimpse of their Chief, he would interrupt his remarks with an apology and quietly slip out to the platform to gratify those who had taken such pains to see him. At one place where several little children had come with the rest he went out alone to take them by the hand, returning with a grave smile on his face and with his clothing covered with snow, and his last act in Bangor, where he stood bareheaded in the rain to thank his old soldiers for their courtesy, was but a characteristic of the true gentility of a President who is one with the people.

President Grant and his party arrived in Portland, from Bangor, between 5:00 and 6:00 a.m. on the morning of Friday, October 20, 1871. The president was received at the depot by Portland's Committee of Reception and taken quietly to the Falmouth House, a large Portland hotel, where apartments had been arranged for the president and his party.

At 9:00 a.m. the presidential procession was formed, consisting of the Portland Light Infantry, Mechanic Blues, Portland Band, Norway Light Infantry and Band, Auburn Light Infantry and Band, Portland Cadets, Army and Navy Union, Grand Army of the Republic. Also included were a large number of invited guests in carriages. The procession proceeded from Falmouth House through the streets of Portland, where private residences were elaborately decorated, to Portland City Hall.

A public reception was given for President Grant at city hall, which was handsomely decorated. Portland Mayor Benjamin Kingsbury, Jr., introduced the president, who spoke to the crowd:

> I have a vivid recollection of visiting your city six years ago. This is the second time I have been in your city, and I am much pleased with the reception here as well as at other places I have visited in your State. If I do not come oftener than I have heretofore, I shall make many more visits here before I am quite an old man.

The crowd was then informed that they could shake hands with Grant, and immediately a jam of people made their way to him. The overwhelming crowd forced the president to retreat out a back entrance of Portland City Hall.

At 12:30 Grant and his party ate lunch from an elegant spread at the Falmouth. At 2:00 p.m. they took carriages for the train depot, where a special train awaited them. The wind was blowing cold and dust, and it was raining. The trip back to the station was uncomfortable.

Two years later President Grant would return to the Pine Tree State. His visit was to be a private, social visit, to Speaker Blaine, who was now the Republican House Leader in Congress. Grant was accompanied by his two sons and his daughter, Nellie. Grant planned no public demonstrations or speeches.

"Of course, the President's contemplated visit to Maine's honored statesman is all that is talked about by those of our people who have not escaped from the heated and sweltering air of the summer solstice," wrote the *Boston Journal*.

The *Daily Kennebec Journal* replied to the *Boston Journal*'s comments, and to constant attacks from a few other national newspapers.

> There are some who are inclined to criticize President Grant for indulging in visits like this. They maintain that he should keep his post at Washington the year round. They seem to be afraid that if

he ventures away from the capital a few days the government will be endangered. They think it improper for the President to seek relaxation or the enjoyment of society, or to put off the magisterial airs of office for the agreeable familiarity of a man among his fellow men. We are pleased to know that President Grant is not governed by such critics or fault-finders but takes a more sensible and proper view of his duties and relations to the people.

The arrival of President Grant in our city to tarry a few days is an event in which our citizens without respect to party feel a high degree of pleasure . . . and when to the dignity of the office the possessor adds the weight of distinguished public service, of patriotism proved and honors achieved in posts of danger and great responsibility, then the President claims gratitude and love for himself as well as the respect due to his office.

The *Bangor Whig and Courier* joined in the welcome:

We wish to add our cordial welcome to those which have already greeted the President's third visit to the State of Maine. The private hospitalities to which he and his daughter and sons have been invited, will be fittingly extended by our distinguished fellow citizen, the Speaker of the national House of Representatives, and throughout the short pleasure tour proposed, both guest and host will be followed by the best wishes of our people, who hold both of them in high esteem for the ability and fidelity with which they have served the Nation.

On August 12, 1873, President Grant's train arrived in Portland on the Eastern Railway at 1:30 p.m., stopping for about ten minutes. In response to the loud cheers from the crowd, Grant stepped out upon the platform of the car and raised his hat in acknowledgement.

Speaker Blaine met Grant and his family on the arrival of the train in Augusta and conducted the party to an awaiting barouche. With Grant and Blaine in one carriage, and the other members of the party in the other carriages, the group made their way through the streets of Augusta, to Blaine's residence. Though a large crowd was at the railroad station and many people lined the streets of the president's carriage, there was no formal parade.

"The close observer would look in vain in his appearance for the evidences of that Caesarism with which one of the leading dailies of New York is charging him in its columns," wrote the *Whig and Courier*. "There is nothing to distinguish his appearance from that of any private citizen."

The following day President Grant traveled to the U.S. Arsenal in Augusta at 11:30 a.m., to be received by Major James Whittemore, who gave the order to fire a salute upon Grant's arrival. The president also participated in a collation provided by Major Whittemore.

The president and his entourage then proceeded to the Soldiers' Home at Togus, where Grant met with the residents and then dined with General William Tilton, governor of the veterans' home.

At 8:30 p.m. President Grant was the guest of the Maine Governor Sidney Perham at the Augusta State House, where a widely attended reception was held for the public in the governor's private room.

On Thursday, August 14, the Blaine's Augusta home was busy with preparations on the spacious grounds. Blaine House, which is now the official residence of the Governor of the State of Maine, is an elegant homestead located near the Maine State House.

Thursday evening First Daughter Nellie Grant was the guest of honor of Speaker Blaine at a reception held at the residence. The Blaines and the Grants had a social dinner at 7:00 p.m., and then shortly after 9 p.m. the tide of Augusta society began to flow in the opened doors. The house was ample in size and was thrown open from hall to library, which enabled the large number of guests to move about with ease and enjoyment. The parlors and drawing rooms were brilliantly lighted and beautifully decorated with choice flowers and wreaths.

It was raining when the doors were opened, but that did not deter the crowd. Speaker Blaine received his guests with President Grant, Grant's daughter Nellie, and Mrs. Blaine on his right. There were a large number of prominent gentlemen with their ladies, principally residents of Augusta and vicinity, though a few invitations had been sent abroad. The company was made up without regard to political bias. There were between 200 and 300 guests.

"The toilets of the ladies were elegant, charming, beautiful," wrote the *Whig and Courier*.

Nellie Grant was richly but modestly attired and was the object of much attention. She was described as having the charming amiability with which she joined in the pleasures of the company, with entire unconsciousness of observation, winning the hearts of all as a lovely American girl.

Blaine's sons Walker and Emmons, described as gentlemanly, assisted in entertaining.

"The host and hostess make entertaining so perfectly a matter of pleasure to themselves that their home is always a home to their guests, and this entertainment in honor of the President and family, while entirely devoid of ostentation, was thoroughly elegant in all its details, and thoroughly enjoyed by everyone of the large number who participated in the Speaker's proverbial hospitality," wrote the *Whig and Courier*.

Adjoining the house, on the south side of the lawn, a large pavilion had been erected, lighted by gas and tastefully festooned with flowers, flags, and streamers, with a smooth floor that invited dancing, while an orchestra in attendance furnished impulse to the dancers and entertainment to all.

"When the dancing began in the pavilion, and chat and flirtation everywhere, the scene was one of great brilliancy," wrote the *Whig and Courier*.

President Grant spent his time enjoying quiet strolls "hither and thither, dignified but affable to all, and seemed to be having as good a time as the rest. There is no immediate prospect of an end of the festivities at this hour, midnight."

President Grant left Augusta by train at 9:00 a.m. on Friday, headed to the coastal city of Rockland, where he was scheduled to travel to Bar Harbor by boat. The train made a quick stop at the railroad station in Bath, where Grant was introduced to the people of that city by Bath Mayor James D. Robinson. President Grant greeted the crowd briefly before the Pullman car was off again.

Hearty cheers greeted President Grant in Rockland, the rain not deterring the large crowd from waiting for him at the wharf. Grant and his party immediately embarked on the U. S. Revenue Steamer McCulloch for the trip to Mount Desert Island. The plan was for the presidential party to spend the night in Bar Harbor and return to Rockland on the McCullough the next day for a trip back to Bangor.

When they left Rockland on Friday afternoon, the weather was quite stormy. By Saturday morning ship had not arrived in Bar Harbor, causing great anxiety.

It would turn out that the fog set in very thick shortly after the president's ship left Rockland, and with the night coming on it was deemed hazardous to attempt to reach Bar Harbor. Instead, the steamer sought shelter and anchorage at North Haven, spending the night there. The ladies of the presidential party were provided with accommodations on board the steamer, while the gentleman landed in boats and found quarters at the house of a Mr. Mullins, who exerted himself to make the men comfortable. On Saturday morning, the trip to Bar Harbor being necessarily abandoned for want of time, the excursionists started directly for Bangor.

At Fort Point, Stockton Springs, a dispatch was sent ashore from the presidential party, and forwarded by telegraph, announcing that the president and his party were safe, and that the steamer would reach Bangor at 2:00 p.m.

By 2:00 p.m. the Sanford Landing in Bangor was crowded with spectators. The streets of the city were filled with carriages and people.

Mayor Joseph Bass ordered a salute for President Grant as the steamer neared port.

The president was received by Mayor Bass, who offered a courteous welcome to Bangor. At once President Grant escorted Mrs. Hamlin and Mrs. Blaine, while Miss Nellie Grant was escorted by Speaker Blaine, to an open barouche. As the carriages of the procession moved off, three hearty cheers for President Grant were given by the assembled crowd. A short detour was made on the way to the Penobscot Exchange Hotel to give the presidential visitors a casual glance at the city, and at about 3:00 p.m. the guests reached the hotel, where a private collation had been ordered by Senator Hamlin.

A large number of people had gathered in front and in the corridors of the hotel, and an eager curiosity was manifested as President

Grant and his companions passed from the carriages to the apartments prepared for them. The interval before lunch was pleasantly passed in chatting over the incidents of the trip, and quite a number of citizens availed of the opportunity to pay their respects to the president and other prominent guests.

At about 3:30 p.m. the party was summoned to the tables, which were spread in the ladies' parlor.

President Grant entered the hotel's parlor with Mrs. Blaine, followed by Speaker Blaine and Miss Nellie Grant, and then the other guests. The room had been beautifully decorated with flowers and vines by the ladies of the hotel, and the tables presented a most elegant appearance, ornamented with choice bouquets, pyramids of sherbet and ice cream, clusters of luscious grapes, and a bountiful profusion of tempting offerings. Thirty-six plates were laid for the presidential dinner.

Senator Hamlin, as host of the occasion, said a few words and toasted President Grant. The toast was received by much enthusiasm.

After dinner, the presidential party headed back to the railroad depot, where a large number of people had gathered. The president shook hands with many who came to the platform of the car. At 7:00 p.m. the train moved out, back towards the Blaine home in Augusta.

On Sunday, August 17, President Grant, his son Jesse, and daughter Nellie attended morning worship service at the Granite Church, with Speaker Blaine and family.

On Monday, August 18, President Grant and the rest of the presidential party left Augusta, arriving briefly in Portland at 11:30 in the morning, on his way to North Conway, New Hampshire.

"All the arrangements of Speaker Blaine have been worthy of the distinguished character of his guests, and the plans for their entertainment during their stay in Maine have been successfully carried out, with the exception of the interference of the fog," wrote the *Whig and Courier.* "We are assured that the President and his charming daughter, Nellie, will bear way with them the pleasantest impressions of their visit to the Pine Tree State, and they take with them the wish of our people that they may soon come again."

4

Chester A. Arthur

President Arthur was here for a day during his administration, but presumably because he was what might be called an accidental president, his presence did not create much of a flutter in society circles.

—*Bar Harbor Record*

Born in Vermont, Chester A. Arthur was a neighbor to Maine. He married Ellen Herndon, became a lawyer, and served as vice president under President James A. Garfield.

In the presidential election of 1880, Chester Arthur wanted to nominate ex-President Ulysses S. Grant. Others in the party wanted to nominate Maine's James G. Blaine. Ultimately James Garfield was elected president, and Chester A. Arthur became president a year later upon Garfield's death in September 1881, two months after being shot by an assassin.

President Chester A. Arthur visited Bangor on September 12, 1882. He had been in Bar Harbor for a day before coming to Bangor.

"President Arthur was here for a day during his administration, but presumably because he was what might be called an accidental president, his presence did not create much of a flutter in society circles," wrote the *Bar Harbor Record* of the president's day on Mount Desert Island.

It was only the night before President Arthur's visit to Bangor that his visit was announced, which caused a stir of excitement throughout the city. General Joseph S. Smith, Bangor's Collector of the Port, immediately started making arrangements for the president's visit.

The Bangor City Marshal sent a police squad to the Bangor House, where President Arthur was due to arrive, to preserve order among the curious throng that had gathered to catch a glimpse of the president. At 6:50 p.m. the carriage carrying President Arthur and his private secretary, Fred Phillips, arrived at the entrance of Bangor House. The president was met there by a General Smith, presumably on behalf of the State of Maine. President Arthur invited General Smith into the hotel, where rooms 42 and 43 had already been made ready for the president, and where a private supper was served.

By now the curious throng in front of the Bangor House had grown into a large crowd, anxious to shake President Arthur's hand when he left for the train station later that night. The president soon acquiesced and spent twenty minutes before supper giving an informal reception, stepping down to the parlor of the hotel, receiving several-hundred men and women, giving a cordial greeting to each person. General Smith introduced the callers to the president. President Arthur took the time to compliment a young lady on her "Tam o' Shanter hat." The president summoned to him a of group of hesitant children who were in the room.

"Come boys and shake hands with me," said President Arthur.

"Everybody was favorably impressed with the bearing and appearance of the president," wrote the *Bangor Daily Commercial.*

After the reception, the police cleared the halls and Mr. Arthur went to his room for a few moments. Soon he walked to room 22 on the second floor for his private supper. Two military officers who had ridden from Ellsworth to Bangor with the president were guests at the meal. President Arthur then emerged through a dense crowd in the Bangor House office and on the sidewalk at Bangor House. The president took a carriage to the Maine Central depot while the crowd gave him three cheers.

The president was due to leave Bangor on a train at 8:00 p.m. Payson Tucker, superintendent of the railroad, quickly telegraphed the railroad's officers in Bangor and instructed them to extend to President Arthur the courtesies of the railroad. Instructions were given to hold the train until the president was aboard.

A compartment in the Pullman car was made ready for the president and a section for the president's private secretary. The party received callers, including members of Maine's judiciary, before leaving the station.

The president expressed gratification at the perfection of the arrangements of his visit.

Benjamin Harrison

I think Mr. Harrison is the person to feel slighted; and those grumblers who are now complaining so bitterly about the matter are the very people who were the least demonstrative on his arrival.

—*Bar Harbor Record*

President Benjamin Harrison traced his heritage back to one of the signers of the Declaration of Independence, great-grandfather Benjamin Harrison. His father, William Henry Harrison, served as the ninth president of the United States. Benjamin Harrison, himself, was a colonel in the Union Army during the Civil War. A native of Indianapolis, Indiana, Harrison was an attorney and served as a United States senator before being elected president of the United States.

Harrison was married to Caroline Scott. He was the first president whose voice was preserved, on a thirty-six-second recording on a wax phonograph cylinder. He installed electricity in the White House for the first time, though he would not touch the light switch from fear of electrocution.

Maine's James Blaine, now with a failed presidential bid behind him, served as President Harrison's secretary of state. Harrison and Blaine were described as being not close friends but still working well together.

The summer of 1889 had been a slow one for the popular Maine summer destination of Bar Harbor. News of President Harrison's impending visit spread quickly across Mount Desert Island. The visit of a United States president was just the shot in the arm the island needed.

"Are you going to see President Harrison?" is one of the most frequently heard questions in several parts of Maine this week," wrote the
Bangor Daily Commercial. "Bar Harbor is making quite an amount of
money out of the Maine people, who are visiting there to see the President. They need about all the wealth they can get to help them out this
season."

During the presidential visit, an embarrassing issue arose in Washington, DC. President and Mrs. Harrison had been accused of break-
ing an engagement with their White House cook and refusing to pay
the wages the cook claimed were owed. The cook contended that she
was engaged by the Harrisons for the entire summer season at the
White House, but when the Harrisons left to travel in the summer,
including the trip to Bar Harbor, Mrs. Harrison tried to save the $50
a month for the cook "when a $15 colored woman would suffice" and
ordered the dismissal of the cook. President Harrison was traveling
without his wife.

Dispatches from Boston before the president's arrival in Bar Harbor
said that the fifty-six-year-old Harrison looked pale and careworn.

On Thursday, August 8, 1889, President Benjamin Harrison was
met in Boston by Walker Blaine, the thirty-four-year-old son of
Secretary of State Blaine. Walker Blaine accompanied his father's guest
on the trip to Mount Desert Island, where the Blaines had a summer
cottage. Maine Congressman Thomas Reed was also aboard the train.

Originally a special train was not going to be ordered, but in the
end it was. The rear car, a Pullman sleeping car, had its entrance decorated and was reserved for the use of the president. The second car,
also a Pullman, was reserved for the use of the rest of the presidential
party. The third car was attached for baggage and additional facilities for
reporters. During the trip President Harrison mostly sat in an armchair
talking to Congressman Reed.

President Harrison's first stop in Maine was South Berwick, to take
on Adjutant General George Sprague and other men from the Maine
governor's staff. Governor Edwin Burleigh intended to meet the train
there but illness intervened.

"On behalf of His Excellency, Governor Burleigh, who is unable by reason of illness to be present to receive you, it devolved upon me to welcome you to our state," General Sprague said to President Harrison. "It gives me great pleasure to welcome you to the State of Maine. May everything conduce to your pleasure and comfort while you remain with us."

The president bowed with a smile to the general. The assembled crowd cheered, hoping to shake the president's hand.

The next stop was North Berwick, where the president shook more hands. A person familiar to Harrison approached the president's rail car.

"How do you happen to be over here," asked Harrison as he leaned over the car rail to shake the person's hand.

"Why, I came over here to find a good healthy country for summer," responded the unidentified person.

At Old Orchard, the president was met by a large crowd, the numbers swelled by summer visitors.

President Harrison's train reached Portland at noon, fifteen minutes behind schedule. While there, Boston & Maine Railroad officials handed the train over to officials of the Maine Central Railroad.

The president was greeted by a great crowd. People filled the platforms and covered the tracks. As Harrison appeared at the rear of the train, a child was lifted up to him. The child had a bouquet of flowers for the president. President Harrison bowed to the crowd before being welcomed by Old Orchard Mayor Holman Melcher, who expressed regret that the president could not stay longer.

In five minutes, after a change of engines, President Harrison was back on his way.

The president was welcomed to Brunswick with a twenty-one gun salute, fired by a platoon from the Maine State Battery.

The presidential train made a brief stop in Gardiner, long enough for a freight train to get out of its way. Lunch was prepared for President Harrison at a table in the president's railcar.

As President Harrison's train traveled through Augusta, he was greeted with an artillery salute.

At Waterville there was an unusually large reception. "This equals Portland," said one presidential staff member. "Yes, and more," replied another.

A little girl offered her parasol to President Harrison, who stood on the rear of the railcar, to shake, as she could not get close enough to the president to offer her hand. In the background a band played.

"When I started, I had firmly resolved to make no speeches," said Harrison to the assembled crowd at Brunswick." "My purpose in visiting Maine, as you well know, is to visit your distinguished citizen and cabinet officer, James G. Blaine."

The crowd roared at Blaine's name.

President Harrison was also impressed with the unusually large reception.

"The preparations you have made here are more suggestive of a speech than any since I have left Washington. I thank you for your cordial welcome and bid you goodbye."

The booming of a cannon signaled the arrival of President Harrison in Bangor. The hour was 3:35 p.m., and the welcoming crowd extended for as far as the eye could see. As the train came to a stop at the railroad station, the crowd engulfed President Harrison's railcar.

"There he is, there's Harrison" called out someone in the crowd, which surged closer to the rear railcar.

As President Harrison was making his way to the rear platform, Vice President Hannibal Hamlin and Maine Congressman Charles Boutelle reached the railcar's steps, coming through a passage that had been made specially through the crowd. Congressman Boutelle attempted to open the door, but it would not give. President Harrison laughed heartily as the glass in the door had to be smashed open by General Sprague to gain entrance.

The president was greeting Hamlin and Representative Boutelle when Mayor Bragg was admitted to the car and was presented to the president. All of President Harrison's guests received a warm greeting.

As the president emerged onto the platform, a twenty-one gun salute began.

Mayor Bragg expressed to President Harrison the compliments of Bangor and her people. He added regret that the president could not stay.

President Harrison then turned to the crowd. Congressman Boutelle prompted the crowd in three rousing cheers. About fifty people had the chance to shake Harrison's hand before the train left Bangor. Two of them were reporters for the *Bangor Daily Commercial,* who "are ready to testify that the President's grip was a warm one."

The crowd was so large that some women got caught in it and begged to be let out. Some fainted.

"I am very glad to have seen you, Mr. Hamlin," Harrison said to former Vice President Hannibal Hamlin as the party exited the railcar. By now Hamlin had retired from public office.

"I am always glad to see you," Hamlin responded.

"He was visibly pleased at the warmth of his reception and expressed his gratification to Adjutant General Sprague," said one of the reporters covering the visit.

The president and his party traveled to the Mount Desert Ferry wharf in Hancock. There, President Harrison was met by Secretary of State Blaine and Henry Cabot Lodge, a United States Congressman from Massachusetts. The presidential party boarded the presidential yacht *Sappho.*

"She was beautifully and tastefully decked with bunting . . . and resembled more a small floating palace than anything in the ferry boat line," wrote the *Bar Harbor Record.*

In Bar Harbor, handbills were circulated announcing the time of the president's arrival. The Bar Harbor Band was stationed near the Bar Harbor wharf, ready to receive President Harrison with fitting patriotic airs. The many fine yachts in Frenchman Bay were decked from stem to stern with flags and streamers. The wharf and shore were crowded with people anxiously awaiting Harrison's arrival.

At 5:45 p.m. the *Sappho* hove into sight around the headland of Sheep Porcupine Island, and as she steamed gracefully into the harbor, the president was given a twenty-one gun salute from the United States Revenue Cutter *Woodbury,* with the smaller vessels in the harbor joining in, the ensigns on the different ships dipped in honor of the president. The band started playing as President Harrison stepped onto the wharf. President Harrison bowed to the left and to the right, greeting the cheering crowd.

A carriage waited to carry the president to Stanwood, Secretary Blaine's cottage. The crowd at the wharf followed the procession up the street. The marching band, with no means of conveyance, fell to the rear. After the informal procession, the welcoming band gave a promenade concert on the lawn of Bar Harbor's Grand Central Hotel.

The party went to Secretary Blaine's cottage, where the Blaine family and a few friends were waiting, with supper ready.

"The president looked as if he needed rest; he was pale and rather jaded looking," reported the *Commercial.*

There was speculation whether President Harrison would tour Bar Harbor's scenic Frenchman Bay. Mr. Walker Blaine, who was in charge of the party program, was described as seeming desirous of leaving President Harrison a margin of choice as to his movements.

Though Harrison's visit was of a personal nature, the *Bangor Daily Commercial* took issue with the lack for a formal welcome for the president.

> The people did their duty nobly; all turned out, either from patriotism or curiosity, to view the chief magistrate of the nation. The pier was full, Main Street was pretty full, and the piazzas of Rodick's and the Grand Central were crowded.
>
> The people about the pier cheered the President, but so studiously plain and unnoticeable was the cortege that the people along Main street were in somewhat of a dilemma to know the Presidential party from its sightseeing followers.
>
> As it is impossible to have a president come here without demonstration, it seems a pity that someone was not authorized to head the occasion. A few people who had flags put them out, and those who cared to indulge in flaunting a bit of bunting here and there did so, but there seemed to be neither order nor motive in the display.

The *Bar Harbor Record* also took the people of the island to task for the president's lackluster welcome:

Did you see the President arrive at the wharf? (I caution you to wait 'til I have got through this paragraph before you answer.) Wasn't it a glorious pageant? The scene itself, one of the most magnificent in the world - beautiful Frenchman's Bay studded with its picturesque rocky islets, in the background the towering peaks of Mount Desert. On the bosom of the harbor the stately yachts, gay with bunting in honor of the occasion; on the wharf, upon the verandas of the hotels, and in groups along the shore, hundreds of the cream of fashionable society interspersed with as many more of the more plebian set from the country villages in the neighborhood. Then, as the pretty little steamer Sappho, draped with the colors so dear to the hearts of all true patriots, and bearing toward his holiday home America's representative citizen, rounded the Porcupine and steamed gracefully into the harbor, did you hear the thundering welcome belched forth from the mouths aboard the revenue cutter? And then, as the Sappho moored to the wharf, and the band struck up a martial air, and the President, hat in hand, stepped down the gangway bowing right and left, did you hear those three cheers which for a time drowned the roar and the band's music . . .

No?: Neither did I; and I was so ashamed of Bar Harbor, and the visitors and the natives, and I wished myself at Newport or some other less fashionable resort . . . at Mount Desert Ferry they gave three cheers and a tiger for the President of the United States; and at Bar Harbor, where nothing had been talked of for a week but the President's visit, the silence was so deathly that the poor man could hear Elijah whisper him to put on his hat or he would get a cold in his head. He ought to have put it on and kept it on till he got to Stanwood! Where was the patriotism of this part of this great Republican state? Where the loyalty of its thousands of visitors? Dried up in the race for the Almighty Dollar, or drowned inside champagne and surfeited with salads. And then, to crown all, the band whose music was to have cheered the President on his triumphal progress to Stanwood, had to walk up, and made a very long tail indeed to the procession. James G. Blaine had little cause to be proud of this part of his State that day. Now. Did you see the President arrive at the wharf?

There had been a rumor circulating around Mount Desert Island that ex-president Grover Cleveland had sailed into the nearby town of Sorrento, and it was hoped that a meeting of the two presidents might boost the island's "lagging summer." It turned out that President Cleveland was not in Sorrento after all.

On Friday morning President Harrison awoke in Stanwood to a hearty breakfast, after which he received visitors. The Blaines took President Harrison on a carriage ride through Bar Harbor later in the morning. The carriage occupied by the president and Mr. Blaine sustained some damage in an accident when turning onto Main Street. In the afternoon, the presidential party went to the cottage of Aulick Palmer, of Washington, DC, for what was supposed to be an informal lunch, but which extended into an evening of lavish entertaining.

Mr. Palmer's cottage was about five miles from the village of Bar Harbor, on the road toward Otter Creek. Two hundred and fifty invitations had been sent out to the cream of Bar Harbor's Summer Colony for the event.

"The dress was elegant and varied, the ladies well represented, although perhaps the matrons prevailed, as was most natural and fit for the occasion," wrote the *Record*.

The grounds of Mr. Palmer's summer home were described as ample. There were eighteen tables spread upon the lawn, with one immense table holding the food and drink. Only President Harrison's table was indoors. Palms, greenery, flowers were everywhere in the rooms and reception halls. Guests poured in and out, exchanging gay greetings.

Among the prominent Bar Harbor summer colonists in attendance were the Vanderbilts, Astors, and people from all over the east coast and beyond "but too numerous to mention." There was a table just for diplomats, along with their large attachés, representing the countries of Italy, Germany, and Russia,

"At the tables outside were represented the social position, wealth, and no little of the beauty of Bar Harbor, although such an affair as this would hardly be so notable for youthful bellehood as some others, a dancing party for example," wrote the *Record*. "No one of note seemed to be omitted.

At President Harrison's table were Secretary and Mrs. Blaine, Senator and Mrs. Hale, Mrs. Palmer, and Mrs. Henry Cabot Lodge of Boston. The floral displays on the president's table were especially beautiful. The centerpiece consisted of tall gladiolas, two hundred in number and variegated colors. At the end of the luncheon the florist, Mr. Fred Moses, presented the arrangement to Mrs. Blaine. Around the room such rare flowers as begonias and orchids that came all the way from Washington "reigned in profusion, regulated by taste." Notable among the floral decorations was a two-foot-long Florida seashell filled with pink pond lilies set in a bank of maiden hair fern.

The food was of the choicest quality, and wines and champagne were plentiful, the champagne described as flowing as free as water. The event was catered by a Bar Harbor veteran caterer known as Sproul. Sproul was said to have been in his glory with the event, keeping a business eye open "against a too lavish use of the punch bowl among guests or waiters."

There was a large number of waiters, many borrowed from the island's hotels due to Sproul's small number of employees. The event began at 1:00 p.m. and lasted until evening.

"The whole affair was on a scale that can hardly be justly described in brief space," wrote the *Record*.

During the reception, Mr. Palmer wanted the president to meet some representatives of the "old regime of Mount Desert." Squire Thomas of Otter Creek was sought. The older gentleman was greeted by President Harrison and others on Mr. Palmer's lawn. The president asked about the older man's childhood and the island.

"His rude, matter-of-fact narrative was listened to with delight by his gracious interviewer," said the *Record*.

The Canoe Club was to host a reception for President Harrison after the Palmers' dinner. Several boats hung with Chinese lanterns and other decorations waited to carry guests to the small Bar Island, directly off Bar Harbor. Women were dressed in white or other delicate evening clothes. The Baldwin Band played for guests, who partook of refreshments that were provided on a grand scale. The event was managed by Mr. Edmund Pendleton.

Rain, however, was threatening the festivities, and President Harrison was too tired to attend. The presidential party stayed home at Stanwood for the rest of the evening. The festivities at the Canoe Club went on without the president.

On Saturday morning the presidential party started on a trip to Somes Sound in carriages, where the presidential yacht *Sappho* awaited.

The residents of the island town of Town Hill were given only twenty-minutes notice that the president would be passing through their town. Flags were quickly found and hoisted. Town Hill residents waved their hats and handkerchiefs as President Harrison and his party passed through.

At Somes Sound, the *Sappho* had been prepared for the occasion. Her cabin was dressed in flowers, and music played from aboard the vessel. On board was the caterer, Sproul, to serve luncheon.

President Harrison was said to look pale that morning. "No doubt the President will enjoy his trip," wrote the *Record*. "Whoever sailed over the dark still watered Sound with its beautiful scenery that did not like it."

The newspaper was wrong, the trip was not enjoyable. Accompanying the president on the *Sappho* were Mr. and Mrs. Blaine and several other officials and prominent island summer colonists. After the presidential yacht left land, the *Sappho* had a hard time in a choppy sea. The fog gave the occupants of the ship nothing to see on land. In a few minutes, stricken with seasickness, few of the presidential party could speak.

"The President tried to keep up appearances but in a short time had to withdraw like any other seasick mortal," said the *Record*. "In short, the Somes Sound trip was a failure."

After arriving at Somesville, President Harrison and some of his party opted to take buckboards home; the rest of the party returned on the *Sappho*.

That evening the president ate in company with his hosts and a small handful of other state officials at Stanwood. After dinner had been planned a grand event at the Kebo Valley Club. At first it was speculated that President Harrison might not recover from his seasickness in time to attend, but he did.

The event at the Kebo Valley Club Saturday night was another splendid affair. Guests began to arrive at nine o'clock. The crowd was estimated to be between five hundred and six hundred people, and they were said to be the cream of Bar Harbor society. Soon the rooms of the private club were filled. A steady stream of ladies moved up and down the stairwell to lay off their wraps while the men entertained themselves in the billiard room. The dresses worn by the ladies were described as remarkable both in variety and beauty.

"To attempt a minute description of them in newspaper space would be impossible," wrote the *Record*. "There were so many of them, they poured in so fast and grouped so thickly together in the moving mass that the rays of a shifting kaleidoscope can best describe the effect."

President Harrison entered the clubhouse shortly after 9:30 p.m. The president took his place near the great fireplace in the reception room, where he spent the greater part of an hour greeting guests. Dancing began then and lasted until midnight.

On Sunday, another controversy with President Harrison's visit to Bar Harbor would arise, this one over the president's choice of church services.

Islanders assumed that President Harrison, a Presbyterian, would be attending services at the Congregational Church on Mt. Desert Street, in the center of Bar Harbor. All day Saturday word had circulated around the small island that the president would be at that church the following morning. Preparations were made. Hopes were raised.

President Harrison never appeared.

Word quickly spread that Harrison, a Republican, had driven some hours earlier to Northeast Harbor, and that he had spent the day with Erastus Corning, of the Corningware business, described by the *Bangor Daily Commercial* as "that rank Democrat."

"This capped the climax of discontent among the disaffected ones," wrote the *Commercial*.

Made aware of the growing controversy, President Harrison quickly issued a bulletin stating that he had not spent the day with

Mr. Corning, although they may have visited, but instead the president went to morning worship at St. Mary's, an Episcopalian church officiated by Bishop George Doane. After church services, Harrison had given an informal reception on the lawn in front of the church and then lunched with Mr. J. T. Gardiner, Bishop Doane's son-in-law.

"This hardly mended the matter" wrote the *Commercial*. "To leave expectant friends of similar religious persuasion and worship in an Episcopal chapel was about as unlooked for as taking luncheon in the house of a Democrat."

At the same time, the newspaper did come to the president's defense. "It did not seem to occur to them that the President had the freedom of motion and the same right to use it as other people, that his time was limited, that Northeast Harbor was an attractive place to look at, and Bishop Doane and Hon. Erastus Corning notable men who have just now several notable people visiting them."

It was said that were it not for the Blaines, the president would not have interacted at all with the public during his visit. The newspaper described the president as generally not wanting to see people and said that Harrison had tried to ride through the streets unobserved. President Harrison had kept his head down when riding in public on the island, suggesting an attempt to escape notice. When he was recognized, however, he bowed his good will on either side in a most gracious manner. Secretary Blaine, on the other hand, was described as a marble effigy that had neither ears nor eyes, staring straight ahead of him the entire way. A member of the Blaine family said they did not want to wear out the president because they wanted him to visit again the following summer.

On Monday, August 13, the president was due to leave on the 10:30 a.m. train for Ellsworth, accompanied by Senator Eugene Hale, to return to Bar Harbor in the evening.

Tuesday afternoon the president witnessed the floral parade at Kebo Valley.

There were thirty-one entries in the parade, all different in color and design. The starting point was the Kebo Valley Club, and after driving around the racecourse three or four times the floral procession proceeded through Mt. Desert Street, Main Street and Cottage Street, at the head of which it disbanded. Mrs. Blaine and Mrs. Cabot Lodge rode in the parade.

President Harrison dined with Mr. W. S. Gurnee at the summer cottage Beaudesert in the evening. After dinner, the presidential party was entertained by a musical performed by amateur actors from the village.

On Wednesday morning President Harrison awoke at Stanwood in Bar Harbor to the patter of rain, which continued throughout the morning while he ate breakfast with friends. After eating, Harrison rode in a carriage for the mile-long trip back to the wharf. The president was wearing a black overcoat over his black frock coat and pants, a black silk hat and brown gloves.

The time of the *Sappho*'s departure was not generally known, but still over a hundred spectators were at the wharf to see the president off. Mr. Walker Blaine was to oversee the president's trip out of the state, but the night before he was hurt in a buckboard accident when he attempted to salute a lady as the buckboard was rounding a corner, leaving him with bruises and scrapes.

Escorted by Mrs. Hale, President Harrison walked from the carriage to the wharf, holding an umbrella over the heads of both he and Mrs. Hale. Closely following him were Secretary Blaine, Senator Hale, Senator Lodge, and several others.

The *Sappho* left the wharf, and then quickly returned. Secretary Blaine was still on the boat but was not traveling with the president, so he had to be brought back to shore.

Due to the cold weather of the day, President Harrison spent the half hour trip to Hancock Point in the boat's salon. In just a few minutes after arrival in Hancock, the president was aboard the train that had brought him to Maine a few days before. The train was decorated with flags and bunting. The parlor cars were decorated with flowers from end to end and from side to side, including gladiolas, chrysanthemums and carnations, ferns and smilax set off in borders of green. On one table were birch bark canoes laden with flowers. The decorating had been done under the supervision of railroad officials.

"I never saw anything more beautiful, and how expressively chaste it all is," said President Harrison.

The train stopped in Ellsworth, where Mrs. Hale departed. The president made a parting word to the assembled crowd there and returned to the train, which reached Bangor at 10:35 a.m. The train was met by an overanxious crowd estimated to be two hundred strong. During the stop, porters stood at the railcars' stairways to deny admittance to the crowd. A man wearing a Grand Army badge and "somewhat under the influence of the ardent" tried to brush past a porter, saying, "I want to go in and shake hands with the general." The porter, an African American man, shook his head and said, "Can't go in there, boss, unless Senator Hale says so."

A young woman from Bar Harbor called to Senator Hale and asked if the president would make an appearance before the assembled crowd.

"Mr. President, let those ladies who are striving to look at your face, see you," said Senator Hale. The senator announced to the people that the president would appear at the rear of the car momentarily, and the crowd quickly scrambled for a spot at the rear of the train.

The president walked to the end of the train, glancing at the newspaper as he went.

"Long live the President" and "Long live General Harrison" were two of the cheers offered. The president raised his hat to everyone before beginning to shake hands.

Quickly people shot up their hands for a handshake, and soon the president's hand was grabbed by the drunk man with the Grand Army badge. The man gave the president's arm a good shake, almost pulling President Harrison off the railcar, leaving one reporter wondering if the president had recovered the following day. (He had not.) The president retrieved his hand as fast as possible and then continued to shake hands, sometimes two at a time.

A reporter said the president looked like he had had no sleep for a week, there was no color in his face, he seemed tired, and he wore a sleepy expression that, however, was said to be particular to Harrison. The president did not smile during the reception in Ellsworth. After the handshaking, the president returned to the interior of the car and sat, with people around him, reading newspapers. The reporter said the president shook hands simply out of courtesy.

The train made a brief stop in Augusta while the postmaster there boarded to greet President Harrison.

Bath was reached about 1:00 p.m. The stores were decorated, and flags flew everywhere. The president was received at the depot and rode through the people-lined streets to the residence of Arthur Sewall on Washington Street, where President Harrison and his party were treated to a formal lunch.

Mr. Sewall owned Arthur Sewall & Co., a shipbuilding yard in Bath. President Harrison was in Bath to inspect her shipyards and harbor.

Traveling from Mr. Sewall's residence to the Bath Custom House after lunch, President Harrison was welcomed on the steps by the children from the soldiers' home. There, President Harrison made the following remarks:

> My friends, my visit to the state of Maine is altogether disconnected from public affairs. I am not here today to speak upon any public topic, only to thank you most sincerely for the cordial manner in which you have received me. I can't, however, leave the presence of these citizens of Bath without assuring them that I have a very deep interest in that industry which built your thriving city, and which has done so much to promote the prosperity of our whole people, the industry of ship building. In every way that I properly can, whether as a citizen, or as a public officer, I shall endeavor to promote the rebuilding of our American merchant marine and the restoration of that great carrying trade which we once possessed in every sea. The arrangements made and the interest I feel in a closer inspection of your shipyards forbid I should speak to you longer, therefore I beg you to allow me to thank you again for your cordial interest and to bid you goodbye.

The president was driven to the works of the southern division of Bath Iron Works, which had been in business only five years and was met by more enthusiasm. The workmen of the building gave a rousing cheer as President Harrison entered and inspected the machinery. Just inside the building were the children of the Military and Naval Orphan

Asylum, the boys on one side of the passage, the girls on the other, approximately seventy children. Each boy held an American flag. As the president entered, the children sang what was described as a very feeling song.

"I thank you, little friends," President Harrison responded to the children.

President Harrison then went aboard the ship *Winona*. She had approximately a hundred guests aboard. Harrison was taken for a cruise, with many other ships following. The president went into the pilot house with some of his friends. Among the sites he saw was the construction of the *Lydia M. Deering*, a new schooner, and shipyards with vessels in all stages of construction.

Under construction at the shipyard at the time of President Harrison's visit was the *Rappahannock*, an American fully rigged ship built by the Arthur Sewall & Co, the business of the president's host. She was launched on January 6, 1890, just a few months after the president's visit. President Harrison donated a portrait of himself to the ship, with the words "May every voyage of the ship Rappahannock be prosperous." The portrait was hung in the *Rappahannock*'s cabin.

Mr. Sewall was encouraged by the president's visit.

> I think that President Harrison's visit to Bath is to make a new departure for Bath enterprise. President Harrison is deeply interested in the development of the American navy, shipping and commerce, and I believe he will be deeply impressed with the capacities of Bath for modern shipbuilding in all its branches. I have invited a number of our Maine representative men to meet the President and join in the welcome and in reviewing the situation here.

Many years after President Harrison's visit to Bath, a reporter who had been sent as a young man from Lewiston to cover the visit shared his recollections with another newspaper.

"President Harrison really came up here to Maine for fun and for rest. . . . Up in Bar Harbor they nearly wore the life out of the President, feeding and entertaining him. . . . [W]hen I first caught a glimpse of the President, he looked tired."

The young reporter had been sent to interview President Harrison on the chances of establishing a naval station at Bath. The president was talking with his secretary of the navy when the young reporter was presented.

> Mr. Harrison was a gentleman. He never forgot that courtesy to all is essential. There are some men of very small position who assume to treat newspaper men cavalierly. The smaller the man— the meaner he usually does treat the newspaper representative, who, in the regular line of his profession, is sent to him to ask questions which he may answer or not but whichever he decides to do still carries with it the demand that he be a gentleman. President Harrison was charming. He was the ideal of true courtesy. He was positively winning in his manner and he answered all of my interrogatories so as to make my heart leap with gratitude.

"And yet he was mortally tired."

At 2:25 p.m. the presidential train arrived in Portland, making its appearance around a curve, and in a moment had passed into Union Station.

For the hour previous to the train's arrival, people had been arriving in a hard rain. Women outnumbered men three to one. The crowd was also anxious to see Blaine, whom, it was rumored, was still with the president.

"[T]here was more desire manifest to see the Maine secretary of state than the western President," said one reporter.

Governor Tom Reed was the first to greet the president. The governor only stayed a moment in the railcar but stayed at the station until the presidential train moved on.

"He's coming," yelled the crowd as the president made his way to the rear of the car, to address the crowd.

"President Harrison looked tired and didn't even bow or smile in response to the hearty greetings he received," said a reporter.

President Harrison shook hands with everyone who could get close enough. An old soldier was given an open way to the president. An African American man made his way through the crowd to shake Harrison's hand. As the train started to pull away, a young lady managed to just touch the ends of the president's fingers. The president then lifted his hat to the disappearing crowd.

"It may be well to add that President Harrison offered his left hand to all who got near him here," said one reporter. "The people at Bath must have been very demonstrative," said the reporter, not knowing of the incident with the drunken veteran a few hours earlier in Ellsworth.

President Harrison said that he had enjoyed his time in Maine, "but his face told rather a different story," wrote a reporter. "He looked worn out, and looked and talked in a listless, dispirited way."

The *New York World* ran a cartoon representing President Harrison indulging in a surf bath at Bar Harbor, with a crowd of office-seekers, in bathing costumes, clustering around him, petitions in hand. Under the cartoon is the remark "Office-seekers pursue him even amid the breakers."

After the president left, at first things were calm on Mount Desert Island.

"Bar Harbor has had a visit from a real live President had has survived it," wrote the *Record*.

> Mr. Harrison's first experience of Mount Desert has been delightful; and how could it be otherwise, with so many of the wealthiest and most influential in society ministering to his pleasure and vying with each other for the honor of entertaining him. Though courted and feted by the gay and fashionable, his courteous dignity of manner has left a profound and grateful impression on the great heart of the people; and the inhabitants of Mount Desert will regard President Harrison's visit to Bar Harbor as one of the most interesting and pleasant events in the history of the island.

Soon, however, honeymoon was over. "How hard it is to satisfy everyone!" wrote the *Record*.

I have discovered, since the President took his departure, that there are a number of people who are thoroughly imbued with the idea that they were slighted by him. I should not be in the least surprised if this feeling finds vent four years hence and the poor man thereby loses the chance of serving a second term. Bar Harbor, during the past two weeks, has been a busy Mugwump factory; and many who cast their vote for Harrison last fall, will be very likely to vote for the opposition next election. If Mr. Cleveland plays his cards well, and takes advantage of his expected visit to Sorrento, he may easily harvest a crop of brand-new Democrats. All that is necessary for him to do, is to make two or three flying trips to this village and shake hands with every Tom, Dick and Harry he meets on the street. . . and whose fault was it, after all? The President seemed willing enough to allow his right arm to be used as a pump handle, and if the citizens of Bar Harbor did not pump, it was because they did not take advantage of his willingness. Surely the very cool reception accorded him on his arrival was proof enough that the people were not very anxious for an introduction or particularly elated by his visit.

I think Mr. Harrison is the person to feel slighted; and those grumblers who are now complaining so bitterly about the matter are the very people who were the least demonstrative on his arrival. But, really, summer is a bad time for any celebrity to visit Bar Harbor. Everybody is busy in the pursuit of the ephemeral dollar. The harvest time is too short to allow of any distraction of that kind, and even the President of the United States is but another drop in the bucket. Still, I don't like to hear people growling and blaming others for the result of their own shortcomings.

The *Bar Harbor Record* also seemed to take offense at the arrival of the national press and the national reporting on Bar Harbor's weather that summer. Such coverage could threaten Mount Desert Island's treasured tourism dollar.

Even newspaper correspondents can be arrant fools at times. The ordinary, everyday Bar Harbor society reporters were not good enough to report the president's arrival, and every large daily was represented on that occasion by specials known as "Our Special Correspondents," in large type. That was all right, so far; but there was no reason why these specials should constitute themselves a Special Weather Bureau and telegraph a lot of lies to their papers concerning the weather at Bar Harbor during the season. The dailies came out next day with headlines in great primer and greater, announcing "A Foggy Season," "The Worst Weather Bar Harbor Ever Saw," "Mid Fog and Rain," and so on. Now the fact is that the weather so far shows a better average than for many previous years, and, in fact, has been fine throughout; but these poor befogged, be-drizzled knights of the pen had become so accustomed at home to the style of weather they depicted that it must become almost a second nature to them, and the fine weather here seemed but a mirage. Still, one knowing their failings, would suppose that they would have discovered it was a dry season at Bar Harbor before they were here over twenty-four hours.

Theodore Roosevelt

I owe a personal debt to Maine because of my association with certain staunch friends in Aroostook County; an association that helped and benefited me throughout my life in more ways than one.

—President Theodore Roosevelt

Theodore Roosevelt was from a prominent New York family. A Harvard graduate, Theodore married socialite Alice Hathaway Lee at age twenty-two. The couple had a daughter, Alice. Roosevelt's wife died two days after his daughter's birth. Roosevelt would remarry, to Edith Kermit Carrow, and together they would have five children. Alice was reported to often clash with her stepmother.

Roosevelt fought in the Spanish-American War. He was appointed by President Harrison to the United States Civil Service Commission, where he fought for reform of the civil service system. In the presidential election of 1884, Roosevelt was opposed to Maine's James Blaine being the nominee of the Republican party.

Theodore Roosevelt served as governor of New York, and he was serving as vice president of the United States when the sitting president, William McKinley, was assassinated.

Roosevelt had been an ill child but grew up to be a robust man, mostly through self-determination. He credited his robustness, in part, to his visits to Maine as a teenager, spending time in the Maine woods with a man who was a registered Maine guide and dear friend to the president.

On August 1, 1902, Bangor Mayor Frederic Boothby announced that President Theodore Roosevelt would be visiting the Eastern Maine State Fair, known today as the Bangor State Fair, on August 26.

Three weeks later, at noon, the train carrying President Roosevelt and his party crossed the state line into Maine.

"President Roosevelt crossed the borders of the State of Maine and entered on the play-grounds of the nation at a season when the summer host is within her borders and when all is festival," wrote the *Lewiston Evening Journal.*

The train carrying President Roosevelt was described as a "gem," made up of the five finest railroad cars that could be found in the East.

The second car in the train was the Thames, from New York City, lent by the New Haven & Hartford Railroad. It was described as the finest dining car known. Two Pullman cars were next, the Umbatilla, borrowed from Jersey City, and the Yale, borrowed from the Federal Express.

Last was the Mayflower, President Roosevelt's favorite car. It was fifteen feet wide and had a drawing room that extended the width of the coach. The car was furnished with fancy chairs, a sofa, and a center table, which gave the compartment a homelike look. It was in that car that the president spent most of his traveling time during his Maine trip. It is where he met with individuals and committees.

President Roosevelt traveled with Owen Brown, his cook, who was African American. Brown always traveled with President Roosevelt. Brown had also been with President McKinley on his trip to Buffalo when that president was gunned down, and Brown accompanied McKinley's remains to their final resting place.

Tuesday, August 26, 1902, was a perfect day. The air was cool and bracing, and not a cloud was to be seen in the sky. A brief thunder shower cleared the summer air in Lewiston and made the weather all the more pleasant for the president's trip.

At every stopping place along the railroad line a great crowd had gathered, and President Roosevelt was accorded a genuine down-east welcome.

"At every stop, he has been received with every possible sign of the devotion of a people not only to the President but to the man—not only to Roosevelt as Chief Executive but to Theodore Roosevelt himself—the ideal of the American people in a thousand ways—the most popular President of the United States in many a year with all classes of people," wrote the *Journal*.

At other places along the rail line, including Hallowell and Gardiner, large crowds stood just to try to catch a glimpse of the popular president.

Old Orchard was Roosevelt's first stop after crossing the state line. Thousands of persons from all parts of York and lower Cumberland counties had gathered in the seaside town, offering President Roosevelt a tumultuous greeting. The crowd was said to be one of the largest ever seen in that town.

President Roosevelt spoke from the rear platform of the Mayflower:

My fellow citizens, men and women of Maine: It is indeed a pleasure to me to have the chance of visiting your great and beautiful state, and I thank you from my heart for the greeting which you have extended to me. In almost every meeting I see men like you, (pointing to a veteran), like you over there, and you, with the boy in your arms there, who wear the button that shows that in the times that tried men's souls, you provided your truth by your endeavor.

In those days Maine was a lesson to all for the way her sons bore themselves in war. Since then and now she is a lesson to us because of the high average of citizenship that shows within her borders, and I think that is the same reason in the one case as in the other the fact that here you have remained on the whole true to the old American theory of treating each man on his worth as a man without regard to the incidentals of his position.

Now you over there (pointing). He was in the great war. (A cry of "Yes" from the crowd.) When you went to war and moved into battle you took an immense interest in what the man on your right hand and your left did, but you did not care the least bit in the world whether they were bankers or lumbermen or farmers or what, if they stayed put. What you wanted was to know that the man had the right stuff in him. And if he had, you

had, you were for him. And if he did not have, you were not for
him. You have got to have the same principle in citizenship. You
have got to apply the same principle in civil life that you may
succeed in the days when you fought because the nation called
you in her distress. The state can do much, but it can't begin to
do everything."

The crowd cried out, "That is right. God bless you. Yes, sir. Amen."

At Biddeford, the train pulled up in the midst of a big crowd at the
railroad station, where President Roosevelt gave a brief speech. The stop
lasted three minutes.

The presidential train arrived at Portland's Union Station at 2:10
p.m., ten minutes behind schedule. President Roosevelt was joined
by Maine senator William Frye, who was acting vice president of the
United States since the assassination of President McKinley. Roosevelt
spoke to a large crowd in Railway Square, after which he was taken for
a drive around the city.

"President Roosevelt is dressed on this tour in an ordinary suit of
clothes," wrote the *Portland Evening Express.*

He wears a black cutaway coat with trousers of a lighter shade and
on his head is the customary silk tile. Perhaps it might be more
appropriate to say "off his head" for the president is not niggardly
in observing the courtesies, although it must be an old story with
him, and his hat is raised a good part of the time. His neck is
encircled by an ordinary turn-down collar held together by an
ordinary blue four-in-hand with ordinary white spots. In dress the
president is certainly ordinary, but it is the personality that tells.
Theodore Roosevelt does not pose as a fashion plate, he poses an
American citizen. He is a man of clean morals and he has no use
for those who are not the same.

While in Portland, President Roosevelt visited the home of a Captain Parker, with whom Roosevelt had served in the military.

"Well, well, Parker, I am glad to see you," Roosevelt said, pump-
ing his arm like a pump handle, excited, with true sincerity. At Parker's

home, the president was served coffee from the old coffee pot that Roosevelt used during the Cuban campaign.

While there, President Roosevelt was presented with a magnificent bouquet given on behalf of the Bosworth Post, No. 2, Grand Army of the Republic. The post consisted of three hundred men and represented every Maine regiment that was in the war. Twenty-six of the men wore the Medal of Honor for gallantry.

President Roosevelt also paid a call at the home of ex-Speaker of the United States House of Representatives Thomas B. Reed at the Longfellow House. The presidential party visited various public parks and other points of interest before returning to the railroad station. Just before arriving at the station, a fervent admirer threw a bouquet of flowers into the president's carriage. President Roosevelt caught the bouquet on the fly with one hand, lifting his hat to the admirer with the other. President Roosevelt and his party left on the train for Lewiston at 4:35 p.m.

The train stopped at Danville Junction, where Postmaster General and Mrs. H. C. Payne stepped on board to greet President Roosevelt. In response to cheers from the crowd, the president said a few words, telling the assembled citizens that their cordiality was characteristic of Maine.

In Auburn, as people waited at the Auburn Maine Central Station, a black cloud grew up in the sky, but quickly turned into a rainbow.

At 5:00 p.m. a barge drove up to the depot in the yard of the railroad station carrying the band of the Second Regiment N. G. S. M., a volunteer military unit of the state, and a few minutes later the police began to rope off the sidewalks and the entrances to the station. At 5:10 the C. Company First Regiment N. G. S. M. arrived at the station and assumed the duty of patrolling the entrances and keeping back the crowds. Marshals on horseback and a squad of mounted police reported for duty, and at 5:15 the crowd of people that had swarmed over the platform of the railway station at its northern end were ordered to find some other place to stand, and the platform was thus cleared for the arrival of the president and his party.

Lewiston Mayor Daniel McGillicuddy arrived in a carriage, soon followed by Mayor Eben Eveleth of Auburn and members of the Committee of Arrangement, dressed in frock coats, silk hats, and gloves.

At 5:46 the whistle of the presidential train was heard in the distance. A minute later the train arrived at the station, drawn by Engine 198 of the Maine Central Railroad.

Upon arrival, a great cordon was brought at once, closing the station to the passing of people. The soldiers kept the crowd at bay, their rifles at their fronts. The train pulled in in such a way that the presidential car stopped at a special platform.

"All happened exactly as ordered. The train pulled up—a face at every window, looking out to see what manner of a town was this," wrote the *Journal*. "They saw a goodly sight, for the sun lay lovingly in upon the green trees and dressed the flags and streamers in all of its afternoon loveliness."

The chief of the Secret Service was the first person to alight from the train, a man described by the *Journal* as having a grim, beardless face, "one of the nobodies of the presidential party whose word is greater than everybody's, a man whose name never appears in the dispatches, who rides on every carriage with the President, and whose eye is on all things pertaining to the safety of the executive."

President Roosevelt was the third person to alight from the train, wearing a silk hat and frock coat, his face opened into a smile that caricaturists loved to play with. Roosevelt stood at the train door for a moment and took in the scene.

A shout went up from the crowd, cheer after cheer. "Hooray for Teddy."

President Roosevelt raised his hat gallantly to the people before being escorted to his carriage, a handsome barouche from a Poland Spring livery. The presidential carriage was drawn by four black horses, white reins attached, which looked striking against the black color of the horses.

The presidential party entered the awaiting carriages, with Roosevelt's Secret Service agent in the president's carriage. They stopped at the gates of the train station and waited for the other carriages to line up, ten or so carriages in all. At 6:00 p.m. the signal was given for the line to start. An uplifted hand by the marshal of the parade opened the way down the streets, "where all was an avenue of the glorious flag we all love so well."

Auburn was beautifully decorated for the occasion. The decorations of the Auburn Engine House were novel and original. They consisted of a big painting of an engine with the smoke streaming from the stack and horses going on a tear. The painting occupied a conspicuous position in the front of and near the roof of the fire station. Directly beneath the painting was a likeness of President Roosevelt. Tastefully arranged streamers of colored bunting completed the decorations.

The decorations of the Auburn City Hall were especially beautiful. The decorators of Lewiston and Auburn had worked all night Monday night.

"When the people went to their work at the office and factory, Tuesday morning, a general transformation had occurred on Lisbon and Main streets. Many buildings whose appearance was bare the night previous, so far as decorations were concerned, were arrayed in the most gorgeous suits," wrote the *Journal*. "Never have we been more proud of these busy industrious cities than this day of welcome," wrote the *Journal*. "For three days, there has been busy work among our people. The entire route of the passing of the presidential party had been decorated with hardly a single vacant place in the line of color along the route. All day Tuesday the people have been gathering. Such an outpouring of the men and women from the homes, the shops, the mills, the farms, and the firesides is rarely seen with us."

President Roosevelt had competition for the crowd in the Lewiston-Auburn area, as the Androscoggin County Agricultural Society's 51st Cattle Show and Fair opened the same day.

"George, of course you are going down to see the President?" asked fair entry clerk John W. Maxwell of one of the farmers.

"No, I can't," the farmer replied.

"Now looky here, have you a decent excuse?" asked Maxwell

"Well, you see, he comes just at chore time," the farmer replied.

"When a farmer won't neglect his chores for a sight of the President, you can be sure the stock in the tie-up is fat and well cared for," wrote the *Bangor Daily News*.

Laborers came from the shops and mills of Lewiston at noon, filling the sidewalks and crossings. Each hour the crowd at Lewiston City

Park thickened and grew denser in anticipation of President Roosevelt's visit. The afternoon trains brought in their supply of people from all directions, eager to catch one glimpse of the president and to hear him speak. The electric cars from East Auburn were loaded with Turner, Buckfield, Minot, and Hebron people. The Sabattus car was packed with representatives from Monmouth, Webster, Wales, and Litchfield. The belt line cars every half hour increased the crowd from eighty to one hundred and fifty each trip. The main line cars brought in Lisbon Falls, Lisbon, and Brunswick citizens. By 5:00 p.m. space on the side-walks had run out, and people were holding their spots until the crowds pushed them inadvertently off them. Police patrolled the area.

"Everyone was peaceable and well-disposed toward his sweating neighbor," said the *Journal.*

Members of the Committee of Arrangements stood upon a plat-form at the park, ready to greet the president and his party. As President Roosevelt's procession approached, a band struck up "Hail to the Chief," and the first boom of a gun from the battery on the shores of Lewiston Falls awoke the echoes.

Roosevelt was pleased with the turnout. He turned to Senator Frye in the carriage they shared and said, "Beautiful, isn't it beautiful. Why, I am delighted with it. Your cities have done so much!"

Every space was occupied by people for as far as the eye could see. Sidewalks, fences, yards and lanes, open windows, rooftops, telegraph poles, all crammed with people. Coe Block was completely covered all along its fire escape with "a bevy of pretty girls."

"Everywhere that the president passed there were cheers on cheers," wrote the *Journal.* Right and left Roosevelt lifted his hat, somewhat the worse for wear, while his strenuous smile gleamed like Ivory all the while."

"Bully for him. He's one of us," shouted a man in his working clothes.

"God bless him! He's a real man," yelled another.

The ride was one continuous cheer, accentuated by the firing of the cannon for the presidential salute.

"It was an unparalleled scene for this city or any other of its size and population," wrote the *Journal.* "From one of the carriages in which the *Journal* representative had the pleasure of riding to look down the street from the top of Court Street hill was like glancing down a double line of waving color of the gayest flag in Christendom backed by the smiling, happy faces of the thousands of men and women who stand behind its dignity and worth."

Besides elaborate decorations, the businessmen of Lewiston had donated between $5 and $20 a piece for the presidential arrival. Local firemen decorated the residence of ex-Mayor N. W. Harris on the corner of Spring and Court street, due to Mr. Harris's illness.

"It was a most touching tribute to the ex-mayor by the boys who love and appreciate him," wrote the *Journal*.

The procession route, a mile between the railroad station and Lewiston City Park, had been cleared of carriages, and automobiles, which were a new invention.

Arriving at Lewiston City Park, a trumpet sounded as President Roosevelt approached the speakers' platform. Women waved their handkerchiefs, and the band struck up "America."

"No improvement in firearms, no perfection of equipment, no change in tactics will avail unless back of them all lies the spirit that sent you and your fellows from '61 to '65, again and again and again against the Confederate lines; that sent you after defeat back again just as if you had won, and after defeat again back again, until from defeat you had wrenched the victory," said President Roosevelt as part of his speech that day in Lewiston.

Roosevelt and his party made its way back down the hill to the Maine Central Station after the speech. While walking to the train, the president stopped and shook hands with a little boy whose father was holding him up to see the president.

At the station, the Secret Service agent who had ridden in the president's carriage visually examined each person boarding the presidential train.

As President Roosevelt entered the train, the crowd was chanting "Hip, hip, hooray!"

The train left at 7:30 p.m., headed for Brunswick.

Accidents were narrowly averted in the crowd of twenty-five thousand people that day in Lewiston. As President Roosevelt was entering his carriage, a man was pinned against the carriage and knocked to the ground. Due to the size of the crowd, several people narrowly escaped injury by trampling.

One young man brought his suitcase with him and stood on it as Roosevelt's carriage passed. The crowd lunged from behind and over went the suitcase. The man, however, did not fall due to being wedged into the multitude. He remained a half a body above the heads of all the others, though now he was fighting to get his feet back on the ground. The crowd shifted its position, and he was borne along with it. His suitcase was being trampled under many feet. The youth was carried out of sight in the distance by the crowd. The remains of his suitcase, pressed out as thin as a flapjack, were discovered after the crowd cleared. An old collar and a faded shirt with a few apples constituted its contents. The apples were transformed into pulp and sweet cider. The shirt and collar were ruined. The man did not return for his suitcase.

"The contrast between this beautiful Tuesday and the day following the death of the man whose position Theodore Roosevelt is now filling with commendation from every person in the United States, was marked. Auburn and Lewiston mourned the loss of our beloved President, William McKinley. The stores and homes were dressed in mourning for him. To-day, the same places are decorated with bunting, pictures of President Roosevelt, the Goddess of Liberty, the Landing of Columbus, and many other features," wrote the *Journal*.

President Roosevelt's train made a brief stop in Brunswick. People started arriving at noon from Freeport, Bath, Lisbon Falls, and from all the neighboring towns. They gathered at the Park Row railroad crossing hours before the train was due, and by seven o'clock it was estimated that there were six thousand people on either side of the track. The crowd was orderly. A large detachment of special policemen was on-hand, whose only job ended up being to keep the track clear.

The St. John Band showed up about seven o'clock and kept the crowd amused. Houses near the railroad station were decorated with Chinese lanterns. On the hill beyond, a collection of fireworks added to the interest.

At nearly 8:00 p.m. the sound of a train whistle was heard. "Here she comes," someone called out as the train came into sight. A great shout went up. When the train stopped, the ropes that were keeping the crowd back were released and the train was mobbed. When Roosevelt emerged, the cheer could be heard miles away.

Roosevelt spoke for just a few minutes, to a very still crowd, who knew the more they cheered the less time they would have to hear the man speak.

"Brunswick has seen President 'Teddy' and everybody is happy," wrote the *Journal.*

President Roosevelt's train made a brief stop in Lisbon Falls before arriving in Augusta at 8:30 p.m.

People had started gathering along the procession route in Augusta long before Roosevelt was expected to arrive. Ultimately the crowd was estimated to be between ten thousand and twelve thousand people.

"Augusta hopes the President is half as well pleased with Augusta as that city is with him. Not having seen the shipping city, the president undoubtedly was fairly well pleased with Augusta!" wrote the *Bath Daily Times.*

Maine's capitol city was heavily decorated. Flags hung off buildings and large decorated portraits of President Roosevelt were in shop windows everywhere. A stretch of the route of the procession had no buildings close to the street, and so was illuminated by torchlight. On the hill, where the area was residential, private homes provided the illumination.

The rooms of the Abnaki Club had been opened to visiting reporters, where every courtesy was shown them.

Shortly after 8:00 p.m. a carriage arrived at the residence of Maine Governor John Hill to take him to the train station to greet the president. As Governor Hill emerged from his house, he was met with a burst of applause from the thousands assembled. As he entered his carriage, someone called out, "Three cheers for Governor Hill."

"They were given with a will, and the popular governor of Maine bowed his acknowledgements of the courtesy so heartily extended," wrote the *Journal.*

At five minutes before 9:00 p.m. the sound of the approaching train was heard. The fireworks from the State House began their launch, giving the signal to the soldiers at the Maine Arsenal to begin firing the presidential salute of twenty-one guns. Two bands were on hand to provide music; one was stationed at the train station, the other at the governor's house. As Roosevelt alighted from the train, the Augusta Cadet Band struck up "Hail to the Chief." As the first strains of that anthem were dying away, the sound of the first cannon shot was heard—the beginning of the National Anthem being its cue.

President Roosevelt was escorted from the train to his carriage. The horse team was driven by Governor Hill's coachman, Andrew Searcy, and the carriage was flanked by mounted police. The procession was organized quickly, and soon the presidential procession was headed to the Blaine House, with the Augusta Cadet Band marching behind and providing the music.

Additional arc lights had been strung up in front of Governor Hill's residence enabling those who could not get within hearing distance to at least get a good look at the leader of the nation.

"As the procession moved down State Street toward its objective point, the scene presented was grand," wrote the *Journal*. "On both sides of the street red lights were being burned by scores of men, stationed here and there by the energetic committee on fireworks; the long strings of Chinese lanterns were aglow, the shouts and cheers of the multitude rang out on the evening air, the fireworks were being discharged on the State House grounds, and the greatest enthusiasm was manifest on every hand."

As the procession passed the Wilbur Opera Company, the members of the opera company were gathered at the side door, leading from the stage, and one of the party fired a revolver in the air, which startled many in the crowd. This visit was only a year following the shooting death of President Garfield.

James Blaine had died nine years earlier, and the Blaine House served as Governor Hill's temporary residence. A small speaker's stand was erected just to the right of the steps of the house for the accommodation of the president and members of the reception committee. The shrubbery had been trimmed for better viewing of Roosevelt.

As the well-known features of the chief executive of the nation caught the eyes of that portion of the crowd located below the governor's residence, the cheers and shouts, which had greeted his appearance above that point, became louder and more enthusiastic. Cheer followed cheer in rapid succession. The president, meanwhile, was rising in his carriage and bowing his acknowledgements to the right and to the left, at the same time gracefully lifting his hat to the crowd.

After arriving at Blaine House, the presidential party reformed inside. President Roosevelt again then appeared at the door. This caused another outburst of applause, which lasted until he began to speak. As the president moved toward the front of a platform that had been erected for the occasion, the volume of the crowd grew louder.

President Roosevelt addressed the crowd.

Governor Hill, my fellow citizens, men and women of Maine, it would be difficult for any man speaking to this audience and from in front of the house in which Blaine once lived (applause) to fail to feel whatever of Americanism there was in him stirred to the depths. (Applause). From my good fortune I knew Mr. Blaine quite well when he was secretary of state, and I have thought again and again during the past few years how pleased he would have been to see so many of the principles for which he had stood approach fruition.

One secret, perhaps I may say the chief secret of Mr. Blaine's extraordinary hold upon the affections of his countrymen was his entirely genuine and unaffected Americanism.

In '61 the easy thing to do was to let the seceding states go. Not only the timid selfish men, but the very good men who did not think deeply enough said that, in addition to the very good men who were faint of heart. That was the easy thing to do, and if our fathers had done it not a man here would be walking with his head as high as he now holds it, for this country would have embarked upon a career both mean and contemptible, a career of being split up into half a dozen squabbling little rival nationalities. We won out because our fathers had iron in their blood, because they dared greatly and did greatly, because when they were convinced where their duty lay, they resolutely did it no matter what the cost.

At the conclusion of Roosevelt's lengthy speech, he and the other members retreated into the mansion, where the president spent half an hour greeting officials.

"It was a grand welcome from a grand crowd to the popular Chief of the American people," wrote the *Journal*, in a story with the headline "Strong and Manly Utterances by a Strong and Manly Man"

President Roosevelt and his party would spend the night at Blaine House as the guest of Governor Hill.

The following morning Roosevelt ate a special breakfast at Governor Hill's residence. The meal featured fresh brook trout that had come from a stream of the Androscoggin River. Governor Hill had commissioned General E. C. Farrington of Augusta, secretary of the Maine Sportsmen's Fish and Game Association, to catch the fish. Farrington had come in the day before on the morning train and fished a stream that he had known for years.

"It is a brook that escapes the attention of the average fisherman, but the general knows its every fall and turn, and from its darksome pools and the edge of its swirling eddies to-day he lured some of the plumpest, handsomest trout that Maine afford," wrote the *Journal*. "General Farrington knows more of the lakes and streams of Maine than any other man and he is one of the men whom the guides say can 'catch fish, even when there aren't any.'"

President Roosevelt and his party left the Blaine House in the morning for a drive around the city before heading to the Maine Central Station in time to leave at 9:30 a.m. for Bangor.

On the drive, the president was driven to the side entrance of the State House, where a stop of five minutes was made to give the party an opportunity for a glance through the building.

Roosevelt was met at the door of the State House by J. M. Libby of the employees' force. Libby opened the door for the president.

"Good morning, comrade, how do you do?" Roosevelt said to Libby.

President Roosevelt spent a few minutes at the State House, hastily passing through the rotunda into the office of the secretary of state, the state treasurer, glancing around each department, and then hurriedly making his exit. He did not have time to go up the stairs to visit the

executive chambers, where several state officials had gathered in anticipation of the president's visit.

The drive then continued up Capitol Street to Sewall Street, up
Sewall to Western Avenue, down Western to State Street, up State to
Green Street, passing Governor Hill's nearly completed mansion.

"This route will show the president as much of the capital city as it
is possible to squeeze into an hour," said the *Journal*. "It takes him by
most of the public buildings, past the homes of nearly all the members
of the reception committee, and it also takes him by the Reuel Williams
house, where President Polk was entertained in 1847."

The party stopped at the offices of the *Kennebec Journal* on its way
through Water Street. Roosevelt was especially interested in the desk
that Mr. Blaine had used when he was editor. Three times the procession was stopped so that children might give Roosevelt a bouquet of
flowers, which were sweet peas. A crowd of people waited at the train
station to give the president a proper sendoff.

Before leaving Augusta, President Roosevelt heard that his friend,
former Registered Maine Guide Bill Sewall of Island Falls, was in Bangor. Roosevelt immediately wired a congressman in Bangor to corral
Sewall and hold onto him until Roosevelt reached that city.

From Augusta, President Roosevelt traveled to Waterville. A stand
had been erected close to the railroad depot there, from which President
Roosevelt greeted a large number of people, many of whom had come
from a distance to hear him.

On the platform the president was presented with a handsome
hatchet with the maker's name attached by a tag, "John King, Manu-
facturer, Oakland, Maine." The hatchet was made especially for President Roosevelt, of the finest materials. On one side was a deer's head
and on the other a sportsman's axe. A portion of the handle was made
to unscrew, which permitted a finely tempered hunting knife to be
unsheathed. Roosevelt appeared much pleased with the gift.

"I passed by your State House in Augusta today," said President
Roosevelt to the crowd in Waterville.

Your legislature only meets every other year. And only stays in session about two months. Quite right. You do not need too many

laws, too much legislation. What we need is stability of laws, fearlessness in applying legislation to new evils, when the evils spring up, but above all common sense and self-restraint in applying those remedies and the fixed and unchangeable belief that fundamentally each man's salvation rests in his own hands.

"My fellow citizens, I wish to thank you, to thank all people of Maine for the way in which I have been greeted. I feel in a certain sense a right to the greeting for at least I am trying to put into practice the principles in which you believe."

The president's train slowed down at Pittsfield and Newport. At each place there was a genuine and hearty enthusiasm. The shouts of the people as the president came out on the rear platform could be heard for some time after the train had gone by.

"He is enjoying every moment of the trip," wrote a reporter traveling with the president.

President Roosevelt's next stop was the city of Bangor, and the state fair.

The fair had opened the day before the president's visit. Officials of the fair and the city had been preparing for the Roosevelt's visit for days. A notice was placed in the *Bangor Daily Commercial.*

To the Heads of the Various Departments of the City of Bangor:

As the President of the United States will be in our city next Wednesday, August 27, out of respect for him personally, and for the high office which he holds, you are hereby authorized to close the city offices during that day.

I am also in hopes that the businessmen of Bangor will close their stores and offices, so far as is practicable, during the President's stay in our city; from 12 o'clock to 4:30 o'clock p.m.

No doubt, in appreciation of the occasion, our people will decorate their homes and places of business, as we wish the Presidential party, also the hosts of visiting strangers who will be with us on that day, to receive such an impression of our hospitality as we think we deserve.

—William Engel, Mayor

The people of Bangor waited until the last minute to decorate for their guest, doing most of the work on Wednesday morning, at an early hour. Janitor Archer decorated Bangor City Hall, which was described as among the best decorated.

The city was decked with flags, banners, and bunting on Wednesday in honor of Roosevelt. "Had Her Glad Rags On" read a headline in a Bangor newspaper.

Between the opening of the state fair and the visit of President Roosevelt, the number of out-of-towners in Bangor that day was estimated to be twenty-five thousand. A record number of people were brought into Maine Central Station in a short period of time, the biggest load being the regular train from Gardiner, Dover, and Foxcroft. Composed of thirteen cars and drawn by two big engines, the train deposited 1,600 people in Bangor. The Bangor & Aroostook from Greenville and Millinocket brought in 1,050 people.

"I never worked so hard in my life as I did between Old Town and Bangor," said a conductor on the Maine Central Railroad.

Passenger steamers such as the *Golden Rod* and the *Tremont* were arriving in Bangor on Wednesday with so many passengers that they topped their weight limits. At the Windsor Hotel in Bangor, people were being turned away before nine o'clock in the morning, and the other hotels of the city were equally full.

The Supreme Court in Bangor adjourned for the afternoon in honor of the visit. The prisoners at the county jail were given a half holiday in the workshop on Wednesday in honor of the president's visit.

The Waterville correspondent of the *Kennebec Journal* said, "Going to Bangor Wednesday?" was now the most common query heard on the street.

"And there are a good many affirmative answers," added the *Bangor Daily Commercial.*

One person who would not be coming to Bangor to see President Roosevelt was his daughter, Alice, though she was also visiting Maine.

Miss Alice Roosevelt was preparing to hold the tiller on a sailboat named the *Raider*, in a sailing competition in the waters between Camden and Islesboro, about fifty miles away from Bangor.

For the race, Alice Roosevelt was to sail from Islesboro toward the Rockland breakwater and back—a distance of about twenty miles—in a Crowninshield twenty-one-foot sailboat owned by her host, Dr. R. H. Derby. The prize was a cup given by Gustavus E. Kessel of New York. Alice was staying at the *Moorings*, Dr. Derby's home.

"Miss Roosevelt is resting to meet the arduous duties of a social nature in Washington this coming winter. In Islesboro she finds perfect rest among her friends and there are no stringent social duties," wrote the *News*.

Alice Roosevelt was described as being an athlete who enjoyed rowing, sailing, golf, and tennis. She was described as a fresh-faced, strong-featured girl, full of life and spirit, and enthusiastically devoted to all that pertained to outdoor life, much like her father.

Wagers were being made in and around Camden and Islesboro as to whether she would win the cup or not. There were roughly twelve boats in competition.

In Bangor, as President Roosevelt was alighting from the presidential train at the Bangor station, someone called out "Three cheers for the President!"

Roosevelt spoke on a platform at the depot, giving a short address. A minute later, he had stepped into his carriage and the drive to Bangor House had commenced. A Secret Service man sat on the president's carriage, which was flanked by mounted police.

On his drive through Bangor, Roosevelt's carriage stopped in front of the Orphans' Home. The children were gathered on the portico, and they greeted Roosevelt with a song, the words especially prepared for the occasion:

"He is very, very good; and be it understood, he is right here in our view."

Roosevelt thanked the children heartily.

"The drive of the President through the city was in the nature of a continuous ovation," wrote the *Commercial*.

The presidential procession went down Main Street at a rapid walk, and the president continually bowed and smiled to the cheers that everywhere greeted him. The drive continued up State Street, around

Chapin Park, through Broadway, back to State Street, up Hammond Street, and out Ohio Street to the Bangor Children's Home.

At the orphanage, a little girl presented Roosevelt a huge bouquet of flowers, which he smilingly accepted. Before the president could leave, another child presented him with the visitor's book and a pen. Roosevelt inscribed his name.

"Bless him," uttered Roosevelt.

The procession headed to the Bangor House and entered through the private entrance of Captain Horace Chapman, the proprietor. Roosevelt then made his way up a staircase and onto the portico in front of the house, where he delivered a short speech to the vast crowd below.

"My fellow citizens!" Roosevelt began. The cheers drowned out his words.

"My fellow countrymen" Roosevelt said, trying again. And again, a deafening cheer.

"It is indeed a great pleasure to be greeted by you today as it has been to be greeted by people all over Maine. I can see by your faces that the old American spirit still burns as freely as ever. Driving through the thronged streets I see men who wear the button which tells that they fought in the great struggle. As soon as I saw the mounted policemen, I knew that some of them were old cavalry men."

"That's right" yelled the crowd, knowing that two of the Bangor police officers escorting the president were veterans of the old First Maine cavalry and of many a hard-fought field.

"You men who fought in that war did the greatest deed which men have ever done. You preserved for us a united country and showed the world that it was ever to be united."

President Roosevelt stopped his speech briefly to ask for his old friend Bill Sewall.

"Now my friends, let me interrupt just a moment. I have a friend here who is lost in the crowd somewhere. He is Bill Sewall of Island Falls, Aroostook County, and if any one does see him please say to him that I want him to come to lunch with me here," said Roosevelt. "If 'Old Bill' Sewall is in town, I want him to join me at luncheon, for I feel like a man who has lost his partner in a crowd.

Earlier in the month, Mary Sewall had looked out the window of her Island Falls, Maine, house, and saw her husband, Bill, hurrying home.

"Theodore is coming to Bangor," said the fity-seven-year-old Maine native to his wife. "He'd like to see us there."

"Goodness, William, I thought somebody died," replied Mary.

On the day before President Roosevelt's visit to Bangor, Bill Sewall dressed in a jacket and uncomfortable white collar and took the morning train to Bangor, to stay at the Bangor House. Mary and the rest of the family would join him the following day.

On the day of Roosevelt's visit, at the Bangor House, Sewall was asked by Llewellyn Powers of Houlton, the congressman for Maine's second district, if Sewall was going to the fair to see the president. Sewall said he would wait for his friend at the Bangor House.

"I want to see Roosevelt," Sewall told the congressman. "If I go down there, I shall not be able to because there will be so many of you fellows around him. I'll be sitting right here."

Later in the morning, Congressman Powers would receive a telegram from the President Roosevelt from Augusta, asking the congressman to corral Sewall until Roosevelt arrived. Again Congressman Powers sought out Bill Sewall.

"The president wants to see you," said the congressman. "He has asked for you in every town in which he has stopped in Maine."

At the Bangor House, the president and his dear friend eventually were reunited.

"I am glad to see you, Bill," said President Roosevelt, whereupon Sewall replied, "You ain't no glader'n I be." Then Roosevelt told the people around him the story of his friendship of many years with the old guide and hunter, and how, many years ago, while on a hunting trip through Maine, owing to the shortage in the meat supply, Roosevelt and Sewall had eaten muskrat together, which the president said was the last meal he'd eaten in Maine before this current trip.

"T'was all we could do to help having a holding match," said Sewall about his reunion with Roosevelt.

"No meeting of two brothers long separated could have been more pathetic than the meeting of the president and the rough woodsman," wrote the *New York Tribune*. "The old man had the day of his life."

"I owe a personal debt to Maine because of my association with certain staunch friends in Aroostook County; an association that helped and benefited me throughout my life in more ways than one," wrote Roosevelt later in his life of his time with the Sewall Family in the northern Maine town of Island Falls.

When he was fourteen, Roosevelt had been sent to Maine by his parents because of a serious asthma attack at his New York home. His parents thought the crisp mountain air of Maine would do him good, and they sent him to Moosehead Lake. It was on this trip that Roosevelt was bullied by a couple of boys in a stagecoach. The experience hurt his pride.

"The experience taught me what probably no amount of good advice could have taught me. I made up my mind that I must try to learn so that I would not again be put in such a helpless position," wrote Roosevelt.

Six years later Roosevelt would meet Sewall, twenty-two years before his visit to Maine as president. Roosevelt was a sickly college student who had just lost his father when he returned to Maine and met the Sewall family. Bill Sewall was thirty-three years old, six foot four, healthy, and strong.

Roosevelt had come to Island Falls, Maine, for Sewall's Registered Maine Guide services. Island Falls was a northern Maine town with a population of 230 people. Bill Sewall, the first white child born in the pioneer town, had just built his house a few years before for himself and his family, which also served as the town's post office and only guest house. Everyone was welcome at the Sewall's.

"As darkness fell on September 7, 1878, Bill Sewall opened the door to find Theodore Roosevelt standing on his porch. Wearing big spectacles and weighing a scant 135 pounds, the Harvard junior looked both boyish and bookish staring up at the tall Maine guide," wrote Andrew Vietze in his book, *Becoming Teddy Roosevelt*.

Roosevelt and Sewall both had endured sickly childhoods. Both enjoyed epic poems and adventure literature.

"Even more central to their bonding, though, they discovered that both were constantly astonished by the poetry of the natural world," wrote Vietze.

To Sewall, Roosevelt appeared as a "thin pale youngster with bad eyes and a weak heart." Roosevelt had been planning the trip for two years. "I feel very sad" wrote Roosevelt in his diary that day.

As the days went on, and Roosevelt began his Maine wilderness expeditions, his attitude, and his life, changed.

"I was accepted as part of the household; and the family and friends represented in their lives the kind of Americanism, self-respecting, duty-performing, life-enjoying, which is the most valuable possession that any generation can hand on to the next," wrote Roosevelt.

Sewall and members of his family would take young Roosevelt on hikes, hunting trips, and camping expeditions through the rugged northern Maine woods. At one point, Roosevelt had to hike down Mt. Katahdin in moccasins after he lost a shoe in a stream.

"I was not a boy of any natural prowess and for that very reason the vigorous out-door life was just what I needed. It was a matter of pride with me to keep up with my stalwart associates, and to shift for myself, and to treat with indifference whatever hardship or fatigue came our way. In their company I would have been ashamed to complain! And I thoroughly enjoyed it," wrote Roosevelt

"I also remember such delicious nights, under a lean-to, by stream or lake, in the clear fall weather, or in winter on balsam boughs in front of a blazing stump, when we had beaten down and shoveled away the deep snow, and kept our foot-gear away from the fire . . . and one meal consisting of muskrat and a fish-duck, which, being exceedingly hungry, we heartily appreciated."

Roosevelt returned to Island Falls at the end of February 1879, just six months after his first visit. The previous trip had done Roosevelt good. School was going better, he was joining in organizations at school, and he was dating Alice Lee of Chestnut Hill, just outside of Boston.

Roosevelt reached Aroostook County by train at 11:00 a.m. Sewall was waiting for him with a sleigh. The trip to Island Falls took all day. The air was frigid. Roosevelt and Sewall had to break the trail much of the way home. But Theodore Roosevelt was happy to be back in Maine. The following day the duo was in the woods, snowshoeing six miles over deep snow.

"I cannot get used to the extreme beauty of the snow-covered pine and spruce forests," Roosevelt wrote in his diary. To his mother, he wrote, "I have never seen a grander or more beautiful sight than the northern woods in winter. The evergreens laden with snow make the most beautiful contrast of green and white, and when it freezes after a rain all the trees look as though they were made of crystal."

On Sundays Roosevelt liked to read his Bible. He went to a place to do it, a point near the south end of Mattawamkeag Lake, near the confluence of the west branch of the Mattawamkeag River and First Brook, where the huge body of water narrows back into a river. Roosevelt returned there many times during his visits to Maine, and the spot is now a Maine Historic Site called Bible Point.

Later in life, Sewall, his brother, and their growing families would go west to help Roosevelt on a ranch he had purchased. They stayed for a few years before returning to Maine.

"Everything so far has gone along beautifully," wrote Roosevelt to a friend. "I had great fun bringing my two backwoods babies out here. Their absolute astonishment and delight at everything they saw, and their really very shrewd, and yet wonderfully simple remarks were a perfect delight to me."

During President Roosevelt's visit to Bangor, Sewall was given a cordial reception by President Beal of the Eastern Maine State Fair. A prominent seat was provided for Sewall on the president's stand.

The fair was the last place Mary saw her husband for a few days. She had returned to Island Falls when, a few days later, her husband also returned. Sewall had accompanied Roosevelt on the rest of his Maine trip, as well as his trip to New Hampshire. Sewall was a hit with reporters from other states.

One national newspaper reporter traveling with the president wrote,

> But Bill Sewall wasn't the whole show, although he did fill a considerable portion of the President's time and thought. He was a

sufficiently large part of it, however, to typify a portion of a speech which the President occasionally delivers, wherein he says that it is not enough for a man to be honest and to be brave, that it is still necessary that he shall have the saving grace of common sense. Bill Sewall has all three of these attributes; hence the honor that was shown him. And the mere act of his participation in today's events is more eloquent of the President's sincerity in his philo-sophical disquisitions on the rights and duties of citizens and the true qualities of manhood, then any spoken words could be. The man who possessed and still possesses the true qualities of man-hood, as outlined by the President, in the three virtues of hon-esty, courage and common sense, and who was good enough to share a boiled muskrat with him sixteen years ago, when he was "Teddy" Roosevelt, was good enough to share with him today a more imposing meal, even though the other participants of that meal were men in the highest councils of the state and nation.

The president seemed to delight in the rural simplicity of the man and insisted that he should sit down to dinner with him. Bill, therefore, had the distinction that seems to come to but few of dining with the chief executive of this nation and the governor of his State at the same time. While at the fairgrounds, someone suggested to Sewall, who was seated on the platform with the president, that he should go to Wash-ington and secure an appointment as postmaster, but Bill had already received this honor and said to his inquisitor, "I be postmaster already."

The following year, 1903, the Sewall Family would be guests of President Roosevelt at the White House.

Wednesday morning had dawned bright, and the weather condi-tions were described as ideal for the great gathering at the East-ern Maine State Fair.

Shortly after breakfast time people began to flock to the park, and from then until the middle of the afternoon the crowds continued to pour in through all of the entrances.

"Maplewood Park never saw such a gathering," wrote the *Com-mercial*. "Besides the thousands from Bangor and the nearby towns, they came from Aroostook and Washington counties from all the stations on the Maine Central and Bangor and Aroostook railroads while a small fleet of steamers helped to swell the gathering by bringing up loads of passengers from river and bay ports. Maplewood was the magnet which attracted half the population of eastern Maine on Wednesday."

Trolley cars hurried back and forth to and from Maplewood Park. Buckboards and public carriages emptied loads of dozens of people at the gates, while hundreds of other people came by private conveyance or walked from downtown. Many Civil War veterans were there.

The decorations at the fair were arranged under the direction of Mrs. H. F. Tibbetts, wife of the chief of police. They consisted of red, white, and blue bunting and evergreen. Several flags draped from the speakers' platform.

Horseracing at the fair was called early. Many families brought with them satchels and boxes with their lunch, and picnic parties were seen all over the fairgrounds. Those eating their lunch tried to finish before the president arrived.

There were many cars at the fair, which was notable in a time when horse and buggy was the most common means of transportation. Most automobiles were being used for advertising, including for the uniquely Maine carbonated soft drink Moxie.

The route through Bangor to the fair was crowded with enthusiastic humanity for the presidential procession, and as the cavalcade of carriages passed, Roosevelt was continually bowing, smiling, and raising his hat.

At the park, someone yelled out "The president's coming!"

All eyes turned toward Main street. "Roosevelt's nearly here."

Escorted by the Bangor Band, the presidential procession entered the fairgrounds through a decorated arch. As soon as Roosevelt's carriage entered the fairgrounds, a great cheer went up.

Hats and flags were waved enthusiastically. Roosevelt showed signs of pleasure at the greeting. He smiled and spoke to President Beal, who occupied the carriage with him, of the enthusiasm of the gathering. Roosevelt's hat was raised repeatedly in response to the cheering and applause.

"It was a hearty welcome," wrote the *Commercial*. "A welcome full of that cordiality for which Maine people are famous. Besides being a greeting, it was a noisy evidence of the high regard in which the nation's chief executive is held down east and of the appreciation which the people have for his coming to visit them."

The carriages entered the track on the northerly side and started around the course, passed the headquarters building, arriving at the platform. The appearance of the president's carriage on the track called forth a thunderous demonstration from the grandstand, where thousands were seated to hear his speech. The cheers could be heard a great distance from the fairgrounds.

President Roosevelt and his party were escorted to the private stand that had been specially erected for the visit. Before the president spoke, he noticed jamming and pushing of the crowd in front of the grandstand. Roosevelt cautioned the people to be careful of the women and children and asked them to show their capacity to manage themselves, which immediately had the desired effect.

Fair president F. O. Beal set the crowd wild when he proposed three cheers "for the noblest president ever heard of."

Roosevelt spoke from a platform that was directly in front of the grandstand, which was packed with people. He humorously informed the crowd that he did not think he faced both ways, but on that occasion, he would have to.

> I am glad to greet the farmers of Maine. During the century that has closed, the growth of industrialism has necessarily meant that cities and towns have increased in population more rapidly than the country districts. And yet, it remains true now as it always has been, that in the last resort the country districts are those in which we are surest to find the old American spirit, and the old American habits of thought and ways of living.

Roosevelt left the platform after his speech to take a ride around the racetrack in response to cries from the audience that he do so. Beal reported that Roosevelt said to him, "It's the best time I've had since I was a young man."

The *Bangor Daily Commercial* summed up the visit in an editorial the following day:

Roosevelt's Welcome to Bangor

The Hon. Theodore Roosevelt, President of the United States of America, has visited Bangor and been given a reception such as no other person could expect to be accorded. The *Commercial* does not feel it necessary to here elaborate upon the meaning of this cordiality upon the part of the citizens of eastern Maine. Their welcome is genuine and sincere. Aside from the mere curiosity of seeing the chief executive of this great nation, thousands of residents of this city and thousands of visitors take this opportunity to pay their respects to the man who, regardless of political beliefs and party affiliation, has commended himself to the whole people as a man in every respect deserving of the high honor accorded him. His record as a public official has been clean; his attitude at all times has been manly and straightforward; his career as a solider, daring, courageous and considerate of his men; his ability as a writer has been universally recognized. Altogether, in the "strenuous" life which he so generally advocates for all young men and of which he is so thoroughly a living example, he has attained that high standard which commends itself to the true American.

Though the president's visit to the fair went relatively smoothly, there were some hitches.

Mr. and Mrs. Freeman Murray of 520 French Street called the police station the day after the presidential visit to ask for help in recovering the sum of $88, which had been stolen from them at Maplewood Park about one o'clock on Wednesday. The couple became jammed in the crowd around the grandstand, and although the pocketbook containing the money was pinned in Mr. Murray's inside coat pocket, it was deftly extracted.

A man named John O'Brien was arrested by a constable and turned over to police on the charge of pickpocketing. O'Brien was thought to be one of three men who took a diamond scarf pin from George

W. Darling of Ellsworth Falls, just at the entrance to the auditorium. One of the men had held a newspaper in front of Darling's face while another extracted the pin. Mrs. Darling, who was standing a few feet away, witnessed the entire transaction. The Darlings were expected to travel back to Bangor to try and identify the prisoner.

When O'Brien was being chased by police, he flung away $41, the exact sum a man had been robbed of in the park earlier in the afternoon. O'Brien had other money on his person. Throughout the day people who came in to report stolen money were taken to O'Brien's cell in an attempt to identify him.

The newspaper reported that there had been scores of complaints from people who had lost money Wednesday. One man complained about twenty cents that had been taken from his waistcoat pocket.

Chief Gilman had ordered saloons in Bangor to be closed at noon, the time of the president's arrival, and that they stay closed until Roosevelt left for Ellsworth at 4:30 p.m. Still, the police arrested more people for drunkenness Wednesday than they had over the past several months combined.

Seventeen people stood in the municipal courtroom. The judge was sympathetic to the event. All but five of the seventeen were released after promising never to again get drunk. The five that were not released were all previous offenders. Those five went to jail.

"They saw the President, but they won't be permitted to witness the Labor Day parade on Monday," wrote the *Commercial*. "But then—perhaps they wouldn't have cared for it anyway."

One of the men admitted that because of the occasion, he perhaps had had a few more drinks than was advisable.

"The court thought so, too, and sentenced him to pound out shore heels in the county workshop for the next fifteen days. He has done it before. They all took their fate philosophically."

After leaving Bangor, the president's train arrived in Ellsworth at 5:45 p.m., on schedule. Senator Eugene Hale introduced Roosevelt to Ellsworth Mayor Arthur Greely, head of the reception committee. Together they walked to a beautifully decorated platform. Senator Hale introduced President Roosevelt to the crowd.

"Mr. Senator, and you, my friends and fellow citizens. I have thoroughly enjoyed the two days that I have spent in your beautiful state. I have enjoyed seeing the state, and I have enjoyed the most meeting what really counts in any state—the men and women," said Roosevelt.

After the president left the platform, he was greeted by an aged lady with an outstretched hand who had not been removed by police. Roosevelt stopped and greeted her. President Roosevelt was said to have had a cordial greeting and smile for everyone he encountered.

As the president waited for departure in his carriage, the crowd was thick on either side.

"Don't get hurt," warned Roosevelt. "Don't get hurt."

A Grand Army veteran took the horse's bridle and passed ahead of the team to keep the people back through the thickest of the crowd, and as the president passed him, Roosevelt bowed and said, "Thank you comrade."

Roosevelt had dinner at the Hale's Ellsworth residence, The Pines. He left at 10 p.m. by train for Nashua, New Hampshire. A large crowd waited at the station, and Roosevelt acknowledged the people with a smile and a bow. After embarking in the rear of the train car, the crowd gave three cheers. Roosevelt appeared at the car's door again.

"Thank you very much," he said to the crowd. "I've greatly enjoyed being in your beautiful city."

Roosevelt remained on the platform as the train pulled out, and with bows and smiles acknowledged the demonstrations of the people.

On the trip to New Hampshire, Roosevelt and Sewall remained awake until a late hour talking over old times. Miss Alice Roosevelt finished fourth in the boat race in Camden.

William Howard Taft

In Bar Harbor war clouds began gathering fast between those residents and the members of the fashionable summer colony whose plans for the entertainment of the president of the United States and the members of his yachting party failed to include any concession to the village folk, of whom there are about 5,000.

P resident William Howard Taft was born in Cincinnati, Ohio. His father was a U.S. attorney general and secretary of war. Taft attended Yale and became a lawyer. He married Helen Herron, and together the couple had three children, one of whom became a United States senator.

In 1884 Taft campaigned for James Blaine's bid for the presidency. Blaine lost to Grover Cleveland as Republican candidate for president.

In 1908, with President Roosevelt leaving office after two terms, Taft was described as being hand-picked by Roosevelt as his successor. Two years after President Taft's visit to Maine, however, he would lose the office during a reelection bid when Roosevelt split the Republican vote by running as a third-party candidate.

Tuesday, July 19, 1910, was the first time a president had come to Eastport, Maine. On that day, President William Howard Taft sailed into Eastport aboard the presidential yacht *Mayflower*. He was arriving from his summer home in Beverly, Massachusetts, to spend a short vacation on the coast of Maine.

The *Mayflower* was a United States naval ship that was assigned for the president's use. The ship was headed for the scrap yard when the Navy bought it in 1902 for $450,000 shortly before the Spanish-American War and converted it into a small cruiser. The *Mayflower* would later become the presidential yacht.

The *Mayflower* was said to compare favorably with the royal yachts of Europe in terms of her size and furnishings. She was 270 feet long and had 2,690 tons displacement. The ship had 170 officers and was commanded by Commander Thomas Snowden. The ship carried light guns, mostly used for salutes. She had been built in Scotland at the cost of $800,000 for a New York millionaire who died before it was complete. Outside she was painted white; inside she was decorated in white, gold, and silver. Aboard *Mayflower*, every provision was made for the comfort of the president and his guests.

The morning of Taft's arrival aboard the *Mayflower* was damp and cloudy, and the air was thick. Eastport Mayor Walter Garnett met the president aboard the yacht as soon as she anchored. Due to an extremely low tide, the yacht stayed out to sea for three hours before the presidential party came ashore.

The presidential party included Taft, his wife Helen, his son Charley, and Horace D. Taft, the president's brother. The entire party had to climb thirty feet from the water to the wharf, up a steep flight of barnacled steps. An old Civil War cannon had been brought to the wharf, and Taft received a twenty-one gun salute.

"It was slow work with the ancient muzzle loader, but the veterans handled the situation bravely," wrote the *Bangor Daily News*.

After coming ashore, Taft spent an hour and a half touring Eastport by automobile. It seemed as though every building in the city was covered with an American flag, the colors of red, white, and blue, and patriotic bunting. Escorted by Mayor Garnett on his sight-seeing tour, Taft displayed particular interest in the sardine industry. The president was presented with a case of especially prepared product.

President Taft arrived to speak in front of the Peavey Library on Water Street. People had been arriving for the event by car and train, and it seemed like all of Eastport was there. Taft was cheered heartily.

My fellow citizens, ladies and gentlemen. On behalf of Mrs. Taft and myself I beg to extend our grateful acknowledgement for this cordial reception. When I was a lawyer there used to be a legal maxim that the proper way to understand a written instrument was to take it up by its four corners, and it seems to me that the same rule applies to the country. The proper way to understand the country is to go to the four corners and the places between.

Taft said that he hoped there would be closer commercial relations with Canada and hoped to establish those relations in the next year. His statement was greeted with loud cheers from the crowd, which held many Canadian citizens.

Taft did not touch on politics in his speech. It was said that state Republican leaders, who had a hard campaign on their hands, hoped that Taft's appearance would boost their campaigns.

In the afternoon President Taft took an auto ride to Indian Point, the farthest northeast corner of the United States. Mrs. Taft and several of her traveling companions visited the Canadian island of Campobello.

The president and his party spent their first night sleeping aboard the yacht *Mayflower*.

While the *Mayflower* was anchored in Passamaquoddy Bay, two Native Americans began paddling their canoe to look over the presidential yacht. The two men stood up in the canoe to have a better look at the craft and at Taft, who was on deck. Suddenly there was a splash as the canoe overturned and only two hats could be seen floating on the water.

Someone called out "man overboard." The boatswain's shrill whistle piped the men of the crew to the lifeboats. Taft himself called out for something to be thrown to the men at once. By this time, the men had resurfaced. One man clutched at the canoe and the other tried to make his way to the *Mayflower*. The *Mayflower*'s lifeboats were quickly lowered. The men were rescued.

The following day, Wednesday, July 20, at 9:00 a.m. President Taft and the rest of his party sailed for Bar Harbor, arriving for a three-day stay.

On Thursday, Taft's first full day on Mount Desert Island, war clouds began gathering fast between the year-round residents of Bar

Harbor and the members of the fashionable summer colony, whose plans for the entertainment of the president of the United States and the members of his yachting party failed to include any concession to the village folk, of whom there are about five thousand.

Bar Harbor Selectman J. E. Bunker, Jr., representing the year-round citizens, said a telegram had been sent to the president while he was in Eastport with an invitation to speak publicly in Bar Harbor, and that no acceptance of the invitation had been received. The Town Fathers felt there was nothing more they could do in the matter.

President Taft was apprised of the situation by the Honorable J. P. Bass of Bangor, who had a summer residence at Bar Harbor. It was suggested that Taft make a speech to the villagers, and Taft consented to the idea. The selectmen quickly agreed to the plan. President Taft then announced his intention to speak to and meet with the year-round residents on Bar Harbor's Village Green the following day.

Details of the speaking engagement were quickly arranged, and placards announcing the event soon were posted at every vantage point and in all but the ultra-fashionable shop windows. Animosity quickly was replaced with enthusiasm at the idea of seeing and hearing the president of the United States.

President Taft spent the rest of his day attending to social affairs, golfing, and taking a buckboard ride to Jordan Pond in the evening for a shore supper of lobster and other sea delicacies. The president and his party traveled for nine miles each way, with a stiff westerly breeze with a whiff of autumn air. The village of Seal Harbor was ready for the president's ride through town.

"In all probability he will be driven through the village proper, so it would be advisable for all to have their bunting and Stars and Stripes ready for Thursday evening," wrote the Seal Harbor correspondent of the *Bar Harbor Record*. "Seal Harbor is one of the most patriotic little villages about here and the President will undoubtedly be given a royal welcome."

The following day, Friday, President Taft suffered a sprained ankle on the golf course at Bar Harbor.

On Saturday morning, President Taft and his party returned to Ellsworth, taking a launch from the *Mayflower* and being met at the Mt. Desert Ferry in Hancock by a group of distinguished citizens, including Ellsworth's own Senator Eugene Hale. Though the president and his party were welcomed by a large crowd, the crowd was not as large as it might have been because a public reception for later had already been arranged.

Taft and his party quickly boarded a special train, for a trip to Bangor.

The special train carrying the presidential party rolled into the Bangor railroad station at noon. As the president's train approached, the city electrician sent a prearranged electrical signal to the station, and instantly pandemonium broke loose. Whistles in the mills and factories along the rivers tooted and screamed; the deep-toned bell in Bangor City Hall tower added its big clamor, and a silvery peal swelled up from a dozen church spires.

In front of the train station was an area that had been roped off and was thickly fringed with police officers. Here sat the presidential touring cars, to take President Taft and his party on a drive throughout the streets of Bangor. For several blocks beyond the barricade, throngs of people waited to see the president. The sun burned down from the sky and the crowd was drenched in sweat. The Maine Second Regiment Band played for the crowd.

Then Taft appeared, and the crowd roared its welcome.

"There were no silk hats and frock coats; the dress of the little party was democratic in its simplicity. Mr. Taft wore a braided cutaway, a white waistcoat and striped trousers; and he looked the picture of rugged, sturdy health, despite a slight injury to his ankle which had forced him on the way up to take ease in a soft-cushioned chair of his private car," wrote the *News*.

The president passed through the gates of the train shed and was promptly greeted by two young women—Margaret Woodman, daughter of the mayor, and her friend Barbara Thatcher. They stepped to Taft's side and pinned a white flower in his buttonhole.

"It was his first taste of Bangor's graceful hospitality, and his lips parted in a pleasured smile as he murmured his thanks and passed on to the city's greater welcome beyond," said the *News*.

The presidential party was shown to the respective cars with remarkable speed and accuracy, owing to the effort of President Taft's military aide, Major Archibald Butt. In the first car rode Taft, Maine Governor Bert Fernald, Bangor Mayor John F. Woodman, Captain Major Butt, Cabinet Secretary Charles Norton, and a Secret Service agent.

Taft made a brief address from the balcony of the Bangor House, where the presidential party attended a luncheon. After visiting Bangor, President Taft and his party headed by special train back to Ellsworth, where they were overnight guests of the Hale Family at "The Pines."

There was no formal welcoming ceremony in Ellsworth, though many turned out in what was described by the *Ellsworth American* as a sincere welcome. Taft spent a half an hour shaking hands.

The presidential party went to Hancock Hall, which housed the city's offices, and which by now was filled inside and surrounded outside by the crowd of people interested in seeing and hearing the president. The building was decorated with flags and bunting. The awaiting crowd was entertained by a band.

President Taft was accompanied by Senator Hale to meet Ellsworth's mayor and other city officials. Due to his sprained ankle, Taft was escorted to a seat in front of the stage to be introduced by Senator Hale:

> "My good friends and neighbors. Ellsworth is highly honored today. It has as its guest the chief executive, the president of the United States and his party, who are visiting Maine, and sailing along the shores. There is no place in the state where the president is not largely and fully appreciated, and there is none among the places in Maine that has a warmer reception for President Taft than has Ellsworth. We trust him today. We welcome him, and, Mr. President, wherever you may go in this state, or in any other state, you will find no place with warmer hearts and people more trustful in you and your great services to the republic than has Ellsworth. I am very glad and proud, my friends, and neighbors, to present the president of the United States."

President Taft spoke to the crowd:

When I spoke to Senator Hale of a plan that Mrs. Taft had for skirting along the coast of Maine, the senator, with his usual courtesy, insisted that we venture inland, at least to Ellsworth. He said it was on the sea, but there were better ways of getting here than with a vessel that measured sixteen feet under water, and so we came around by Bar Harbor and have had the hospitable reception that one always gets at the Hale household.

It is a great pleasure to be here and to meet the people of Maine—the people who make the strength of Maine and have given her the standing she has in the Union. Where there has been a cause for patriotic service for the country, Maine has responded with all efforts and all courage. It gives me great pleasure to come to Maine, to your beautiful city of Ellsworth, and see this arched street of elms.

President Taft then became part of a receiving line, and people started to file though to shake his hand. Taft then left the hall with Senator Hale and returned to The Pines, where Hale hosted a dinner party in the president's honor.

Taft spent what was described as a "delightful" Sunday in Ellsworth. The day began with a visit to worship services at the Congregational Church. Services at that church originally were not going to happen that Sunday, as the minister had just started his summer vacation. However, Taft expressed an interest to Senator Hale in attending church, and Hale quickly got in touch with Reverend R. M. Mathews, who consented to delay his summer vacation and reopen the church for a special Sunday service for the president.

The service was to begin at 10:30 a.m. The doors opened at 9:45, and at 10:15 the building was full. The church had been decorated with simple but unique decorations. The large mahogany pulpit of the old church was covered with festoons of clematis and jardinieres of pine, and large vases of dark red poppies were used to good advantage. Maurice Rumsey was at the organ. Miss Bertha Giles was the soloist. The music was provided by a mixed quartet.

Taft entered the church promptly at 10:30 a.m., and the assembled crowd inside stood in unison. President Taft occupied the Hale pew with Mrs. Hale and the president's brother. Directly behind them was Senator Hale. Also in the party at church were Mrs. Taft and Major Butt, among others.

Reverend Mathews delivered the sermon, based on I Corinthians 2:16. At the end of the service, the audience remained standing as Taft and his party exited the church.

At 1:00 p.m. Taft and his party were driven in automobiles to Senator Hale's camp, Nicolin, for luncheon. The party spent the early afternoon at the camp with Senator Hale's company. At about 4:00 p.m. the party returned to Ellsworth, and at 4:30 p.m. they boarded the special train for Mt. Desert Ferry. As soon as the president was aboard the *Mayflower*, she weighed anchor. She stopped briefly at Bar Harbor for mail, then headed to Islesboro.

The *Mayflower* spent the night at sea in a heavy fog. She reached Islesboro Monday for a brief stop. President Taft went to Rockport, where he was a guest at luncheon of Cincinnati friends, and the *Mayflower* then returned to Islesboro for the night. Mrs. Taft's sister, Mrs. Thomas K. Laughlin, of Pittsburgh, was spending the summer at Dark Harbor, and the purpose of the trip there was for the two sisters to visit.

The next day President Taft visited Rockland, and in the afternoon went sailing on Casco Bay.

During Taft's visit, he was accompanied by Major Archibald Willingham Butt, forty-three. Major Butt, a former reporter, had served in the Spanish-American War. Taft first knew Butt in the Philippines, where Butt was stationed. Later Butt would become a military aide to Theodore Roosevelt and then President Taft.

At each place visited by President Taft in 1910, Major Butt was the man first met by Maine officials, and who finally settled all plans for entertainment. Because of the nature of a presidential visit, plans were constantly changing. With all that responsibility, Major Butt had even found time to take Mrs. Taft shopping while her husband was attending to official duties.

Butt ingratiated himself with the Maine people during that visit. When Taft and his party arrived in Eastport, Maine, on Monday,

July 18, 1910, Major Butt ensured that the party was efficiently distributed into the proper automobiles. He was praised for his tact and for
the easy way he handled the arrangements.

Two years after President Taft's visit to Maine, Major Butt perished
in the sinking of the *Titanic*.

"All those who met him on his visit to Maine in 1910 became very
fond of the man, and their sorrow at the news of his sad fate at sea
would be that of men and women who have learned of the death of a
personal friend," wrote the *Lewiston Evening Journal*. "At times, not only
in Eastport, but at the other places visited, it became necessary for him
to change the plans of local committeemen, but the way in which he
did it caused no bitterness, and made all feel that he was one of the best
sort of men they had ever met."

Major Butt was forty-five when he died on *Titanic*. The purpose
of his trip to Europe in the first place had been to take a rest from his
duties in the nation's capital.

After news broke of *Titanic*'s sinking, one of the early visitors to the
White Star Line offices was Taft's brother, Henry Taft, who came asking
for tidings of Major Butt, on behalf of his brother, the president. Tele-
graphic inquiries were made to *Carpathia*: "Rush definite news whether
Astor, Butts, or Guggenheim on *Carpathia*."

Miss Marie Young, formerly of Washington, had been a special
music instructor to the children of President Theodore Roosevelt and
so knew Major Butt well:

> "The last person to whom I spoke on board the *Titanic* was Archie
> Butt, and his good, brave face, smiling at me from the deck of the
> steamer was the last I could distinguish as the boat I was in pulled
> away from the steamer's side," said Miss Young. "Archie himself put
> me into the boat, wrapped blankets around me, and tucked me in
> as carefully as if we were starting on a motor ride. "Goodbye, Miss
> Young," he said, bravely and smilingly. "Luck is with you. Will you
> kindly remember me to all the folks back home?"

A writer for the *Washington Star* who witnessed the scenes of the
New York dock Thursday night, says it was the unanimous statement

of not less than a dozen women with whom he talked that the heroism and the gallantry of Major Butt left a deeper impression upon their minds than the disaster to the steamship or their own personal experiences, awful as they were.

"Major Butt was the highest type of officer and gentleman," said former President Roosevelt. "He met his end as an officer and a gentleman should, giving up his own life that others might be saved. I and my family all loved him sincerely."

"Major Butt was my military aide. He was like a member of my family, and I feel his loss as if he had been a younger brother," said President Taft. "I cannot enter a box in the theatre, I cannot turn around in my rooms in the White House, I cannot go anywhere, that I do not expect to see his smiling face and hear his encouraging tones. The life of a president is rather isolated, and those who are appointed to live with him come much closer to him than they would filling a similar function for other persons." The consequence is that the bond between an aide and a president is very close."

In October of 1912, when news of a possible second visit by President Taft reached Augusta, the State Superintendent of Schools wired the president an invitation to meet and address Maine teachers during the annual meeting of the Maine Teachers' Association:

Portland, Me.

To His Excellency, President Taft, Beverly, Mass.

The knowledge having come to our notice that on Oct. 23 you are to pass through Portland on your way to Poland Springs, and the fact that the Maine Teachers Association with an expected attendance of 2500 or 3500 teachers is to convene in our City Wednesday, Oct. 23 to Friday, October 25, and that the citizens of Portland are uniting with the 7000 teachers of the State of Maine to make this convention an unprecedented success, we extend you an invitation to address a few words to us. We suggest that the opening session on Thursday at 9 a.m. will be an acceptable time, as a recital on our new municipal organ occurs then, but any time during the convention which may be named by you will assure our plans being made in accordance.

The invitation was accepted on behalf of President Taft, but only two days before the president's visit to Maine.

Citizens were urged to turn out for the president's arrival, regardless of political beliefs.

Governor Plaisted directed the issuance of special orders granting permission to the Portland companies of the Coast Artillery Corps and the two Portland divisions of the Naval Reserve to parade the following day as escort to President Taft while he was in the city.

The president's visit to the teachers was non-partisan. However, Taft was in the middle of a difficult reelection campaign. The popular former president Theodore Roosevelt, once a champion of Taft, had thrown his own hat in the ring to return to his former office. With news of President Taft's visit, attendance at the teachers' conference was record-breaking.

"Every topic of conversation today has given way to the discussion of the coming of the President, and everywhere, whether at club or social affair, presidential possibilities were discussed, for some who the prospect of seeing the head of the nation made everyone realize how very near is election day and the interest in this event is by no means confined to the members of the male sex, even in Maine, where women have not the right of suffrage," wrote the author of the "Social Gossip" column for the *Portland Evening Express*.

On Wednesday, October 23, 1912, President Taft received a warm welcome from the same newspaper:

Portland welcomes the Chief Magistrate of the Nation.

It honors the great office which he has so successfully held for almost four years, an office honored before this time by the greatest names in history, a list to which impartial historians will surely add his own name.

It honors the man. He has been an upright citizen, a great judge, a gentleman with an unsullied record, and is a patriotic, high-minded, able, and distinguished President.

Portland is pleased with the opportunity to pay its respects both to the man and to the President, and proud that he honors it with a visit.

Its every gateway is wide open to him and he has the keys.

With one accord its people salute the chief citizen of the land.

Taft spent the morning playing golf at the hotel in Poland Springs. It was a rainy day, and there were intermittent showers and a continuous fog. President Taft was drenched when he and his golf party arrived back at the hotel, and he had to change clothes before leaving for Portland.

President Taft was originally going to arrive in Portland by car. The rain and the resultant muddy roads quickly changed the plans, and the president and his party was forced to travel by train.

Five carloads left Poland Springs for the train station. The last car did not make it to the station on time and the train had to be stopped so the latecomers could board. Many towns along the way were disappointed by the change in plan, having made plans and placed decorations for the presidential drive-by.

President Taft and his party arrived at Union Station in Portland about 3:00 p.m. from Poland Spring. Taft's train was met by a reception committee of representative citizens, which formed an escort through the city to Portland City Hall.

Along the way about six hundred children from the Kavanaugh School stood in the rain in front of their school on Congress Street and waved American flags as the president drove by. President Taft waved his hand in return at the children. At Portland City Hall, Mayor Oakley Curtis introduced President Taft: "Mr. President: A most pleasing duty has devolved upon me, in my capacity as mayor of the city of Portland, to render to you the people's acknowledgement of your affording us this short visit, and we extend to you a most hearty greeting and cordial welcome."

President Taft addressed the crowd.

I am greatly touched by your generosity and hospitality of your welcome. Under the circumstances, I appreciate it most heartily. . . . I am glad to be in the state of Maine, because of what I know of Maine people. When I was first introduced to the politics of the nation, it was at a time when a man had to respect Maine politicians if he hoped to be anything at all. . . . Why did everybody have to recognize these men? Simply because the Maine people put good men into office, and they kept them there until they became accustomed to their duties and were a help to the whole country.

At the conclusion of his speech, a huge key bearing the word "Portland" was presented to Taft.

The president was ushered into the mayor's office and then through to the reception hall, where he received a few prominent Portland people. There was a reception at the Portland Club at 5:15. The women of the presidential party were entertained at the Lafayette Hotel while the president spoke at the convention.

"President Taft appeared happy, and his familiar smile brightened and broadened frequently during his trip," wrote the *Express*. "He was quick to appreciate the humorous incidents, and the human side of his nature put everybody at ease and relieved any suggestion of embarrassment that interferes in functions of this sort at times."

As President Taft, whose brother was a teacher, took the stage to give his address to the teachers' association, he was given a loud, positive greeting. The teachers in the crowd waved tiny American flags. Lorenzo Moulton, the president of the Maine Teachers' Association, told the crowd that he had made President Taft an honorary member of the association.

After the president's speech, the organist led in the anthem America, with everybody standing and singing, and President Taft joining in.

"It was a spectacle that would make the most sluggish blood race through the veins and cause the throat of a stoic to choke up with emotion," wrote the *Evening Express*.

The streets were lined with people as Taft left Portland, to take the train back to Poland Spring, where he spent the evening quietly resting.

On Friday, the presidential train stopped again in Portland, briefly, where the president's private car, the Ideal, was switched to the 12:05

train for Boston. The president did not leave the car but appeared on the rear platform for a moment to bid farewell to Honorable Arthur Sewall of Bath, a personal friend, who had also greeted President Harrison twenty years before. Mrs. Taft and her daughter went into the station briefly to purchase magazines and "dainties."

"The President leaves the State of Maine strengthened in the popular esteem and enriched with a new admiration for him even among those whose conception of political duty leads them to feel that they must vote against his retention in the Presidential office. That he should come to our City at this time, in the midst of the stress of political warfare, come as the guest of the City, entirely apart from political considerations, and receive the welcome that he had without any regard to political lines, is testimony both to his worth as a man and to the quality of our own citizenship," wrote the *Evening Express.*

Warren G. Harding

What a glutton president Harding is for work. If he calls his little outing of last week a vacation, what pace must he set when he works!

—*Portland Evening Express*

President Warren G. Harding lived in rural Ohio all his life. He was a newspaperman, and it was in that role that Harding supported Maine's James Blaine as the presidential nominee in 1884. President Harding would die two years after his visit to Maine. His death was attributed to a cerebral hemorrhage. Former President Taft would follow Harding's casket in the funeral procession, immediately behind the casket, along with the new president, Calvin Coolidge.

President Warren G. Harding was fifty-five years old when he passed through Portland on Tuesday, August 2, 1921, on his way to a vacation in the White Mountains of New Hampshire.

The president's Maine pass-through disappointed the people of Westbrook, where President Harding had been expected to stop. The city had been decorated and plans had been made. But for naught.

President Harding tried to make up for the slight when he motored from Mt. Prospect, New Hampshire, to Poland Springs, Maine, the afternoon of Saturday, August 6. The presidential party spent the afternoon in Poland Springs playing golf and then headed to Portland and Westbrook. The Westbrook City Band entertained the crowd until the president arrived about 8:45 p.m. and briefly addressed the citizens of Westbrook from Riverbank Park.

In Portland, President Harding visited a hospital and talked for a few minutes to each of the patients.

The presidential yacht *Mayflower* sailed from Portland about 10:00 p.m., with Harding expecting to be back in Washington no later than Tuesday.

Due to the personal nature of President Harding's trip, not many details are known. It would appear that he was busy during that trip, as evidenced by an editorial in the *Portland Evening Express.*

"What a glutton president Harding is for work? If he calls his little outing of last week a vacation, what pace must he set when he works!"

Franklin Delano Roosevelt

The thing about Maine people is that during the summer, they fish and make babies. During the winter they don't fish.

—President Franklin Delano Roosevelt

Franklin Delano Roosevelt was the second legendary President Roosevelt to visit Maine, thirty-four years after his cousin, Theodore. Franklin D. Roosevelt was the thirty-second president of the United States. He was elected to that office four times and died while in office. Roosevelt's legend grew from his management of the Great Depression and World War II.

Roosevelt, who was fifty-four years old at the time of his first visit to Maine as president, was born in Hyde Park, New York. He married a distant cousin, Eleanor Roosevelt, and together the couple had six children. The Roosevelt family had a home on Campobello Island, New Brunswick, Canada, a Maine neighbor. It was at Campobello Island that Roosevelt fell ill with polio, spending the rest of his life walking with heavy, clumsy assistive devices on his legs.

In the summer of 1936, President Franklin D. Roosevelt had not planned on visiting Maine when he and his family made their way to Campobello Island for a summer vacation. Quickly moving events surrounding the Passamaquoddy Tidal Power Project, Quoddy Village, and the way the projects were quickly bankrupting neighboring Eastport, Maine, changed the president's plan.

The Passamaquoddy Tidal Power Project was an idea to harness the great tidal strength of the Cobscook and Passamaquoddy bays to feed turbines that would generate electricity. Franklin Roosevelt had endorsed the idea in a speech given in Eastport in 1920, when he was a vice presidential candidate.

After the stock market crash, in 1935, President Roosevelt allocated $7 million from the Public Works Administration to build two dams across Cobscook Bay, and other structures, including permanent and temporary housing at a nearby property—Quoddy Village—located in Eastport.

Facing much opposition, including from the southern states, the project was not re-funded, and work stopped in August 1936, a year before Roosevelt's visit to Eastport as president. Eastport was heavily invested in efforts to bring industry and much-needed jobs to the area based on the project.

On Tuesday July 28, two days before Roosevelt's visit, the Public Works Administration released their list of funded projects, and Maine was among eleven states omitted. This meant no further funding for Quoddy.

Secretary Ickes was asked why Maine had not been included.

"Now, what do you want for Maine?" replied Ickes. "We gave you Passamaquoddy."

Ickes said there would be no further funds for Passamaquoddy.

"Eastport continues to hope doggedly that something will be said or done to save the dam," wrote the *Portland Evening Express.* "They understand the dam project. They have lived on plans for "the dam" for years. When it came, or started to materialize, they didn't look upon Quoddy as a form of relief, but as the fruition of a dream Eastport had cherished for nearly a decade. They still want the dam, above everything else. They know little or nothing about any other form of relief, and they scoff at the talk of converting Quoddy Village into some sort of a settlement camp. "What is resettlement?" they ask. "It's just a large-scale poor farm, isn't it?"

The talk in a desperate Eastport was the possibility of Quoddy Village being taken over and made viable by some other branch of the United States government. All eyes in Eastport turned to Campobello Island, and President Franklin D. Roosevelt, who had been the champion of the project. He had promised. He was their last hope. People were starting to feel frustrated and angry, and reelection was getting near.

A rumor began circulating that the National Relief Agency might take over the project. On Tuesday night National Relief Administrator Harry Hopkins denied he had announced any definite plan for taking over the village and said that if such an announcement was to be made, it should and would come from the president.

"Nevertheless, the rumor persisted here today, and Eastport was wondering just what it might mean for the future," wrote the *Evening Express*. "Eastport bigwigs today cautiously evaded commenting when the *Evening Express* asked for their opinions on the possibility that W. P. A. or some other branch of the National Relief Administration might "take over" Quoddy village."

When Roosevelt visited Campobello Island in July of 1936, it was uncertain up until the last minute whether he would visit Quoddy Village. A visit had been planned for Tuesday, but the president did not arrive.

At the same time he canceled his visit on Tuesday, President Roosevelt sent an invitation to Eastport's leading citizens for a picnic at Campobello. That invitation was seen as Roosevelt's way to compensate the people of Eastport for canceling his visit, thus quashing hopes that he would tour Quoddy, and possibly save it.

"Maybe they can get a cheering word or two out of the big boss then," said the *Evening Express*.

The following day, after greeting their Maine guests at Campobello, the president sat on a blanket, surrounded by his wife and mother, who sat on cushions and blankets. Other family members roasted sausages over a wood fire arranged by sailors from the Potomac and the destroyer Hopkins. Royal Canadian Mounted Police in uniform added an international flair to the event. The president talked with the premier and the attorney general of New Brunswick.

This was a rare opportunity in which photographs were allowed, and hundreds were taken. At a press conference on the beach FDR was surrounded by a score of newspaper men from all over the United States. Roosevelt called it informal.

President Roosevelt referred to the Passamaquoddy Tidal Power Project as a laboratory that presented great possibilities for future power development. He spoke of two other places in the world that were experimenting with tidal power, and he said if Quoddy was successful, it would be just the first of many tidal power projects.

Roosevelt said that if Canada would work with the United States in harnessing the Bay of Fundy tides on the New Brunswick side, there stood the possibility of a free exchange of surplus electricity between the two countries. The president cautioned that he could not proceed without the approval of Congress, but he still tried to hold out hope.

"Quoddy will be completed," said Roosevelt.

The *Bangor Daily News* printed an editorial that detailed the uncertainty surrounding the Quoddy project:

> Just how, he did not make plain. . . . At his press conference on the beach at Campobello early Wednesday afternoon, President Roosevelt declared flatly that no more money could be spent on Quoddy unless authorized by Congress. No two ways about it. A remarkably definite expression for him . . . but, from the front porch of his cottage later in the day, the President told a group of Island people and Eastport neighbors that he believed they would see Quoddy completed.
>
> "We are going to have Quoddy," he told 150 people he had invited to an informal reception on the lawn.
>
> At the informal reception of Eastport, Lubec, Calais, and Machias people who paid their respects to the president before the doors of his summer home, the chief executive said, "Quoddy will be completed, there will be some delay but that is necessary to educate the people of Canada and the United States to its possibilities. Some parliamentary and congressional action may be necessary before that is accomplished. I believe in Quoddy."
>
> Hundreds of Quoddy residents hungry for some word of the future of the project drew a deep breath of relief and a shout of joy pierced the fog and near rain through which they had come to hear what the president had to say regarding their bread and butter of the next year or two.
>
> If you're good at jigsaw puzzles, try to fit those several pieces together. . . . The answer seems to be that Mr. Roosevelt was on another excursion into dreamland. This time he saw the United

States and Canada collaborating in a vast international power development, embracing the whole border from Quoddy to the Great Lakes.

Despite the picnic at Campobello on Wednesday, President Roosevelt had not formally refused the idea of a visit to Eastport. That city had been abuzz all morning Wednesday wondering if he would or would not visit Eastport.

Maine newspapers made calls to the Secret Service agents on Campobello Island, the Army engineer in charge of Quoddy Village, and other presidential officials, only to be told that no one knew if a visit was going to happen.

At noon on Wednesday, Wilford S. Alexander, head of the Federal Alcohol Administration, made the announcement that Roosevelt and his party would be visiting Quoddy Village that afternoon.

"That ought to be straight; I got it myself from the President last night," said Alexander.

After the announcement of the visit, it was decided that no formal celebration be planned. Oscar Brown of the Eastport Chamber of Commerce told the *Portland Evening Express* that Roosevelt was regarded as an old friend and that the town would respect his implied desire that there be no demonstration when he motored through.

"We're going to have the band out, but that's all," Brown told the newspaper.

Shortly after the announcement of the visit, the town was suddenly draped in American flags and was said to have a holiday appearance. Bulletin boards were quickly covered with signs that urged the largely Republican Eastport to "vote for your city's best friend."

On Thursday, July 30, 1936, President and Mrs. Roosevelt rode into Quoddy Village at 4:50 p.m., beneath sunlit yet cloudy skies, to the cheers and tumultuous reception of more than two thousand people.

The president's visit was on short notice, yet there were five hundred cars full of people to greet him, coming from miles around. The president had also made the trip to Eastport by car, across the harbor by car ferry, to Lubec, and then to Quoddy Village, a distance of forty or fifty miles.

The president stopped at the exhibition building and inspected the working model of the tidal power project.

Pausing in the doorway to the exhibition hall before entering, the president tried to give Eastport hope.

"When I come back next year, I hope it will be going," said the president.

Police held the crowd back as the presidential party headed for town in their vehicles. The president's car was driven by James Mullins, a young man from Eastport who was the regular driver for officials at Quoddy Village.

The procession made its way around the historic Carrying Place, where Native Americans used to carry their canoes in order to avoid the long journey around the southern end of the island. From there the presidential party could look down upon the homes of the officials who had built Quoddy Village to its present state. They could see the general layout of the most important section covering the year's work.

The presidential procession then went into town. The USS *Potomac* awaited the president for a trip to St. Andrews and Quebec. Hundreds of cars kept arriving, sirens blew, people waved and shouted greetings to the president.

In Canada, President Roosevelt was expected to discuss with Canadian Premier MacKenzie King hydro-electric power at Quoddy and on the St. Lawrence River.

The day after President Roosevelt's visit, it was announced that 250 employees would be laid off that day from the Quoddy project due to work drawing to a close.

"Wait a few days and you'll find out what they're going to do with Quoddy's model village and all its grandfather clocks, silk bedspreads, and love seats," wrote the *News*.

Are you dizzy? If the situation appears to you as a trifle obscure and the prospect somewhat less than satisfying, just remember that as a wholesale dealer in hopes deferred Mr. Roosevelt is in a class by himself. And don't forget his advice to "cling to your dreams." Not very filling, to be sure, but often diverting.

Though Roosevelt won the election again that year, Maine's electoral votes did not go to him.

President Franklin D. Roosevelt's second visit to Maine was just four months before America's entry into World War II. Germany had invaded the Soviet Union and was marching across that country at the time of the president's visit—more of a stop—in Rockland.

Two weeks before unexpectedly turning up in Rockland, Roosevelt sailed aboard the presidential yacht *Potomac* from New London, Connecticut. On board with Roosevelt was Major E. M. Watson, secretary and military aide, Captain John R. Beardall, naval aide, and Rear Admiral Ross T. McIntire, surgeon general of the navy and the president's personal physician. President Roosevelt was reported to be on a fishing trip. This trip had been the first time FDR had not taken along representatives of the country's top newspapers. There was a news blackout regarding the president during that period, the first in the modern era.

On August 14, 1941, two days before Roosevelt's visit, word came that William Hassett, one of the president's confidential secretaries, would arrive in Rockland from a nearby vacation spot, which was a tipoff to reporters that the president would be arriving soon. National news correspondents started arriving in Rockland rapidly as reporters from major newspapers flew in from Washington or hurried from nearer points by train.

Hassett met with reporters in Rockland the next day and said he had received the following message from the president, who was aboard the *Potomac*: "Potomac is anchored near Deer Island, Maine, and has on board Hopkins, Watson, Beardall, McIntire, and myself. We land tomorrow and take train to Washington, arriving sometime Sunday morning. All well."

Hassett told reporters that President Roosevelt would land at Tillison's Wharf in Rockland sometime the following afternoon, completing a cruise during which he held a historic conference with Winston Churchill, the prime minister of Great Britain.

Rockland was chosen as the landing point because it was one of the largest sheltered harbors on the East Coast and had a direct rail link to

DC. This was the same wharf where President Roosevelt had ended his 1936 visit to Maine.

Colonel E. W. Starling, chief of the Secret Service White House detail, met with local officials. In Rockland, Deputy Marshal A. P. Richardson told reporters that the Secret Service had advised city officials to expect the president after lunch. The president ultimately arrived earlier in the day.

The Maine State Police sent fifty troopers, and fifty deputy sheriffs were expected to report for duty for the president's visit, including many sworn in specially to function under the civil defense program for the day. All law enforcement was ordered to report at 11:30 a.m. for duty guarding the president's route from the waterfront to his special train.

The new Ocean House in Rockland served as the headquarters for the press corps during the visit.

For two hours on the morning of Friday, August 16, 1941, fifty newspaper and radio reporters waited in the big freight shed of what was once the Eastern Steamship Company. From that group, twenty-five reporters were invited to be received by President Roosevelt in the cabin of the *Potomac*.

"We all but stood upon each other's shoulders," said reporter Oscar Shepard.

On the *Potomac*, President Roosevelt sat at his desk, dressed in light tweeds, described by Shepard as "brown as an Indian, and seemingly in fine health, he impressed those who saw him for the first time by the vitality and youthfulness of his appearance. He looked at least 10 years younger, here in the cabin of the Potomac, than ever he has appeared in the newsreels."

Shepard said he was also impressed with what he called the Roosevelt personality.

"It seemed to flow from him."

The president smiled at the reporters as they gathered, greeting the Washington correspondents by name. Mr. M. E. Hennessy of Boston, the oldest reporter present, sat beside the president at his desk, at Roosevelt's request. Henry Hopkins, who had been involved with the Quoddy Village issue five years earlier, had joined the presidential party and stood behind Roosevelt but said nothing.

President Roosevelt announced that he and Churchill had met aboard the British ship *Prince of Wales* and the American ship *Augusta*. Roosevelt was asked whether America was "any nearer to the war." Roosevelt hesitated a moment and then replied that in his opinion we were not. A reporter asked if the president could be quoted on that. The request was refused.

Roosevelt said he would like to have slain his confidential secretary, William Hassett, for revealing that the presidential yacht was headed to Rockland.

"But the flashing Roosevelt smile in Hassett's direction robbed the words of any sting."

It had been foggy between North Haven and Rockland the afternoon of the president's visit. Roosevelt said that even though the *Potomac* had been on the open sea, no torpedoes had been launched at her.

"The President said this unsmilingly. Was it a touch of whimsical humor or a warning in grim earnestness?" wrote Shepard.

Roosevelt emphasized the need to discuss more openly the possibility of the Nazis winning the war and dominating the world, and what that would mean.

President Roosevelt also spoke at length about a Sunday church service held aboard the *Prince of Wales*.

Shepard described the conference as tense and quiet.

The Maine reporters remained silent as the national reporters dominated the press conference, always referring to President Roosevelt as "Sir." Jim Moore covered the visit for the *Portland Press Herald*. Moore said that Sidney Cullen, a reporter for another newspaper, was physically escorted off the presidential yacht because he had attempted to bring a camera aboard. Cullen was allowed to return without the camera. The room in which the informal meeting took place was below deck and was hot and steaming. Roosevelt was relaxing in an easy chair, smoking a cigarette in his customary long-stemmed cigarette holder. He told a joke about Maine people.

"The thing about Maine people is that during the summer, they fish and make babies. During the winter they don't fish," Moore quoted the president as saying, many years after the 1936 visit.

Moore explained why he did not ask questions of the president.

"If I could have thought of anything world-shaking, I would have asked him. But I couldn't think of a damn thing."

The entire meeting with reporters lasted for twenty minutes and was entirely off-the-record.

The president's special train came in at 9:00 a.m., hauled by Engine No. 463. She had been shined up for the special occasion. The train had ten cars—one Maine Central baggage car, six regular Pullman cars, one New Haven Railroad dining car, one observation car for the president's personal use, and the private car Ronald Amundsen.

The president's trip from the wharf to the train was about a quarter of a mile long. The route was closed to traffic. The president was expected to board the train at Broad Street because there was not enough room to place a ramp along the special train.

According to Theodore W. Sylvester, Jr., co-author of *Home Front on the Penobscot Bay: Rockland during the War Years*,

As kids we were pretty much isolated from the war. When President Franklin Roosevelt visited Rockland in 1941 on the eve of the war, the fact that Rockland was featured on the movie screen was big news. My recollection of the Roosevelt visit was a giant parade and hordes of people everywhere. I took up a position at the railroad station to try and get a glimpse of the President. As the train pulled away from the station, with Roosevelt standing on the rear platform, I ran up the tracks to get a better look.

If you ever see that old newsreel, and there's a kid dressed in knickers running up the track, I claim that I was that kid. Nobody believed me at the time, however.

Dwight D. Eisenhower

I'd better be careful, my pockets are crammed with all kinds of fishing flies.

—President Dwight D. Eisenhower

President Dwight D. Eisenhower was sixty-four years old when he visited Maine—twice within a month, in 1955.

Eisenhower had served as a five-star general during World War II. In 1951 Eisenhower switched political parties, from Democrat to Republican, and ran for the office of the presidency a year later. In that office, he fought the war on Communism. Eisenhower was the first president covered under the Twenty-Second Amendment to the U.S. Constitution limiting the terms of president at two. Future President Richard M. Nixon served as Eisenhower's vice president.

As part of a six-day tour of northern New England, President Eisenhower took a three-day fishing trip to Parmachenee Lake, in the Rangeley Lakes region of western Maine, almost on the border of New Hampshire.

President Eisenhower was officially here at the invitation of fellow Republican Maine Senator Margaret Chase Smith. The president's visit was stated to be non-political, though he would be running for reelection the following year.

"[M]any Republicans join the Democrats in smiling a bit at the report that Mr. Eisenhower's visit will be 'non-political,'" wrote Lorin L. Arnold in an editorial for the *Bangor Daily News*.

"On behalf of the people of Maine, I extend the warmest welcome to the President and have placed all our state facilities at his disposal, in the hope that his visit will be a happy and repeated one," said Democratic Governor Ed Muskie. "We are looking forward with a great deal of pleasure to the visit of the President."

On Saturday, June 25, 1955, in Rangeley, Maine, the national and local press corps were transported to the remote area in special cars and buses. *Bangor Daily News* reporter Lorin Arnold and outdoor writer Bud Leavitt, along with photographer Edward Baker, traveled in a bus operated by Patrick I. O'Connell of Bangor, who was said to be the Bangor and Aroostook Company's safest driver of the past three years. Sergeant Guy Batchelder of the state police was assigned to record film of the trip.

On Saturday, when a tired-appearing President Eisenhower arrived at the landing, he saw that reporters were already there.

"How did you fellows get here so quickly—did you fly?" asked the president.

President Eisenhower stayed at the Parmachenee Lake Club, which was located in the Maine wilderness about fifty miles from Rangeley. The cabin in which the president stayed was called the "Little White House" for the weekend. White House Press Secretary James Hagerty was flown from Washington to Rangeley Lake House in a Maine Fish and Game Department plane.

The presidential party was accompanied by Miss Maria Doukas of Lewiston and Allan Callahan of Auburn. Doukas was the National Committeewoman from the Maine for the Young GOP, and Callahan was editor of *The Trunk*, the monthly publication of the Maine Young Republicans.

"We believed we should come along on this trip to get material for a report for the Young Republicans as to how the president looked," Miss Doukas told a reporter from the *Bangor Daily News*. "We have been behind him from the very start and still are."

Constantly at the president's side on the lake trip were seven "trim-looking" state police officers, who were assigned to be at President Eisenhower's side until he left from Dow Field in Bangor on Monday night.

The state police detail on hand for the visit was under the supervision of Lieutenant Roger Baker, commander of Troop C., Skowhegan. The detail included Sergeant Kenneth Twitchell of Farmington, and troopers Carl Buchanan of Skowhegan, Frederick Kneeland of Clinton, Herman Holbrook of Waterville, Lester Farrar of Rangeley, Wilfred Tufts of Kingfield, and Stephen Wentworth of Wilton.

On Saturday night President Eisenhower and others were enjoying a game of bridge in their wilderness cabin. At 9:00 p.m. the game was interrupted by a very important call with international consequences.

On Wednesday, an American plane had been shot down between Siberia and Alaska by America's opponent in the Cold War, the Soviet Union. Both the United States and the U.S.S.R. issued conciliatory statements regarding the shootdown, and over the following days tensions slowly eased.

President Eisenhower talked on the phone with his secretary of state, John Foster Dulles, from Little White House. It was originally agreed that the president and Dulles would discuss the matter when Eisenhower returned to Washington on Monday night. Ultimately, due to the urgency of the situation, Dulles would fly to Dow Air Base in Bangor Monday night to meet the president and fly back to Washington on the same plane, allowing them time to discuss the situation before the president's return.

The president's press secretary was asked about the incident.

"They had an interesting game of bridge during the evening," Hagerty told reporters. "The President's present reaction is that he wants to confer with Secretary Dulles as quickly as possible."

The following day—Sunday—President Eisenhower was up at 7:30 a.m. and had a breakfast of tomato juice, bacon and eggs, and coffee. Leavitt said the president ate baked beans for breakfast, lunch, and dinner during his stay. Eisenhower was said to have personally thanked the camp cook after every meal.

Eisenhower was kept inside by a heavy downpour in the morning, but just before noon the sun started to come out and warm up the area.

"He lost no time getting into fishing togs," reported Leavitt. "It was evident from the start that Ike wanted to go fishing."

Eisenhower was accompanied on Sunday's fishing by his chief aide, Sherman Adams. They traveled two and a half miles up Magalloway River to Rump Pond, a 150-acre body of water situated close to the river.

The fishing party arrived at the boat landing at 2:14 p.m. Eisenhower stepped from his heavily guarded limousine and hurried down a thirty-foot approach leading to a newly lumbered dock. While walking on the landing the president put his hand in his coat pocket and stopped suddenly.

"I'd better be careful, my pockets are crammed with all kinds of fishing flies," said Eisenhower.

At the wharf, President Eisenhower was introduced to seventy-year-old Arthur P. Merrill, a guide at the Parmachenee Club. Eisenhower greeted Merrill warmly, shaking his hand with firmness and pleasure.

Within a few minutes Merrill skippered the president across the short 300-yard strip of water to the Parmachenee Club.

"In less than an hour the president was standing on the slippery rocks at Little Boy Falls, Magalloway River, making long, effortless casts into the glistening, untroubled waters of the trout-rich pool," Leavitt wrote.

Presidential aides said that if Eisenhower's casting skill had any fault, it was because he was suffering from a case of bursitis. Leavitt said the president's casting skills did not appear impaired at all.

"The President is catching fish fast and furiously!" said Eisenhower's press secretary.

The president capped off the day of fishing by landing an eighteen-inch salmon weighing approximately three pounds. That was going to be part of his breakfast the next morning. Sunday night the president spent the evening again playing bridge with a small group of friends at the Parmachenee Club.

President Eisenhower was noted by Leavitt to be the first active president ever to fish Maine waters while in office. A large portrait of Eisenhower in fishing gear was drawn for publication in the *Bangor Daily News*.

On Monday President Eisenhower spent the last few hours at the camp having a "bull session" with Maine's Republican leaders and national party leaders, including Maine's three congressmen. Eisenhower was said not to have talked politics during his visit, though others reportedly did.

Before leaving the Rangeley area, the president was presented with a fawn for the children of the nation's capital from the children of the Rangeley Lakes region. The fawn's name was Bambi II. She was presented to the president by Candy Tibbetts, the thirteen-year-old daughter of Mr. and Mrs. Verde R. Tibbetts of Rangeley.

Bambi II had wandered into the yard of a resort on wobbly legs. She had been fed and cared for by Jerry York, son of the resort owner. The children of the area asked if she could be presented to President Eisenhower. The director of the National Zoo in Washington assured the youngsters that Bambi II would be taken care of nicely and that all the children of Washington would have a chance to see her as soon as she arrived.

Eisenhower was described by reporters covering his visit to the Rangeley Lakes region as having been changed by the visit. They said they felt he had loosened up.

"For instance, we were permitted to get real close to the president when he did his first fishing in Maine Saturday afternoon and everybody had ample opportunity to shoot pictures of him," said one national photographer who followed the president regularly. "But before, under similar situations, we've never been able to get within three feet of him. That's a big change." He seems to be more relaxed on this trip and sometimes acts like a candidate for re-election."

The president was described by Leavitt on his second day as being relaxed and bronzed to a healthy shade of moccasin brown.

"Maine hospitality for the President's visit was complete in all respects—with one exception," wrote Leavitt. "The black flies and minges took full liberty with the presidential anatomy."

Leavitt said that insect repellant did not help the president. The Secret Service got the worst treatment from the blackflies, said Leavitt. He told of what an agent from Alabama said when he showed Leavitt the markings left from the blackflies.

"I sho' never did see nothing like them things in 'Bama. Lord, how they chew ma hide!" quoted Leavitt.

Driving from Rangeley to Skowhegan, the presidential convoy encountered little highway difficulty. "Ike never missed a chance for a wave," wrote Leavitt. "Small clusters of folks, twos, threes and four in a group, waved and he never missed an opportunity to greet them."

Crowds jammed the town curbs at Rangeley, Farmington, Norridgewock, Skowhegan, Canaan, Pittsfield, Newport, Carmel, and Hermon. At each place, the president slowed up the convoy and waved a greeting.

A tiny, gray-haired lady sat on her lawn in a wheelchair awaiting Ike's convoy at Detroit. When the president passed in his limousine, he stood and seemingly gave the lady a personal greeting. The long, black vehicle passed, and Ike continued to wave to her. Tears welled in her eyes.

"The memory of the President giving her a personal greeting will live forever," said Leavitt.

Toward the conclusion of the Maine trip, one Secret Service agent praised the people of Maine.

"These people are wonderful examples of real Americans. A job like this, of course, is quite complex. Yet, these folks helped make it fairly simple. Their sincerity was beyond reproach and so very much appreciated," the agent said to Leavitt. "But those no-see-um mosquitos, even the Secret Service couldn't compete with those pests."

Skowhegan, the president's destination, was "bedecked in President's Day finery," ready to greet the president, who was expected Monday afternoon to make a major address at the Skowhegan State Fairgrounds before being a guest of the legendary Maine Senator Margaret Chase Smith, who lived on Norridgewock Avenue.

Traffic directions were posted around Skowhegan Monday. There was no traffic allowed on the streets the presidential procession would travel.

The presidential procession entered the main section of Skowhegan across a bridge bedecked with an American flag. Another flag greeted him stretched across Water Street, the main thoroughfare. The motorcade proceeded on Water Street to North Avenue, then to Chandler Street, to Madison Avenue, Beech Street, and the fairgrounds.

Church bells, sirens and whistles accompanied the cheering throngs who lined Skowhegan's streets. Banners, bunting, and flags lined the route of his motorcade.

"The reception at Skowhegan was nothing short of amazing," wrote Leavitt.

People started gathering at the Skowhegan Fairgrounds at 11:00 a.m. on Monday. Fair officials were planning for between five thousand and fifty thousand attendees at the Skowhegan State Fair that day when President Eisenhower arrived.

Stores, factories, and government buildings in Skowhegan were all closed at 3:00 p.m. so that all local residents would have an opportunity to join in the president's greeting. The Loring Air Force Base Band, the Brunswick Naval Air Station Band, and the Skowhegan Senior and Junior High School bands entertained fairgoers while waiting for President Eisenhower's arrival.

In the car with the president when it reached the fairgrounds were Senator Smith and Governor and Mrs. Muskie. As President Eisenhower alighted from the car, he paused before the Honor Guard and received four ruffles and flourishes from the Loring Air Force Base band, followed by the National Anthem. Eisenhower stood erectly as the band struck up "The Star-Spangled Banner."

"This was an impressive moment as all military personnel stood in salute and the civilians paid the customary tribute with the men putting their hats over their hearts and the women placing their right hands over their hearts."

The cheers were deafening as the presidential party made its way to the speakers' platform. Reverend John F. Johnson, pastor of the Bethany Baptist Church, gave the invocation, while the benediction was given by Reverend Lucien Chabot, pastor of Notre Dame de Lourdes Church. President Eisenhower was first greeted by Governor Muskie.

"It is with very great pride that I welcome you, Mr. President, to Maine," Muskie said in his greeting.

"There are those who might suggest that you should feel more at home in Maine than I, despite the fact that I was born in the state," said Muskie, a Democrat, of the largely Republican state of Maine. "But, we would like to have you return here annually—whatever your occupation. It is a sheer pleasure to rub shoulders with such a warmhearted human being as you have proved to be. May you have a warm spot in your heart for us and our hospitality."

Governor Muskie presented the president with a carved wooden eagle.

"This is a small token of our affection for you, Mr. President, and we hope it will find a place on your Gettysburg farm as long as it is a part-time or fulltime home."

The crowd roared with approval.

The carved wooden eagle was sculpted by John Upton of Bremen, an internationally known sculptor, "who got sick of the city life and came to Maine to live," said Muskie.

When Senator Smith spoke, she praised President Eisenhower's part in bringing peace to Korea. She said Eisenhower "has brought our country the greatest degree of peace we have had in many years—in fact, almost in twenty years. What greater tribute could be paid to a man?"

Senator Smith presented the president a gift for himself and his wife, Mamie, which was a small pine tree neatly planted in a small flowerpot.

"We hope you will place this on the White House lawn and in 1961 replant it on your Gettysburg farm." Her remark drew laughter, with its implication that the senator hoped the president would run for, and win, a second term in the White House, not leaving until 1961, instead of 1957.

A tourmaline bracelet was presented to the president, a gift from the people of Bar Harbor for Mrs. Eisenhower. President Eisenhower addressed the crowd at the fair: "From the bottom of my heart, I thank you, the governor for his official welcome, Senator Smith for all that she so extravagantly said about my accomplishments, and each of you for the courtesy you have paid me by coming out here today that I might say hello. No man can receive greater acclaim than to be received in friendly fashion by a gathering of real Americans."

Eisenhower said his visit was long overdue and that his education was not complete without making acquaintance with the people of New England. "I have satisfied a long-felt desire to come here. I am grateful for the warmth of the welcome I have received all along the line, from young and old, from men and women, from workers and people who seem to be on vacation."

The president added:

My real word of thanks is this: that you have let me feel that you do stand with one another shoulder to shoulder and also shoulder to shoulder with other localities and states and regions of all the states—that all of us, together, may march along to that fuller life, strong, secure but tolerant and ready to help the other fellow, as we expect him to do his part in this great venture.

I can't reach each of you personally with a shake of the hand. I cannot even speak to all of the citizens I saw today. But if you, and through you, I could let each of you know how sincerely I appreciate the warmth of your friendliness, how earnestly I want to come back, as your governor said, no matter what my job may be—then indeed I shall be content.

In his remarks, President Eisenhower emphasized that the goal of America should be the winning of permanent peace and not just the cease of gunfire, and that sacrifices are always required for such a mission. He said there could be no prosperity without peace. Before concluding his remarks, President Eisenhower acknowledged his Maine visit with the blackflies.

"And I might say the most touching welcome that I received was from what the guides call midges but which I call plain black flies. I am certain that during all three years when I did not come to Maine, they have been waiting for me, because they swarmed around me with their cannibalistic tendencies, and I am sure they will probably starve until I get back here."

After the president and his party had left, at the end of the evening there was much extra trash, which was burned. The fire got out of hand and the fire department had to be called. The fire was extinguished quickly.

On that Saturday, while the president was traveling from Rangeley to Skowhegan to attend the fair, Senator Smith spent the morning of the visit getting things ready at her home.

"I'm just doing what any woman would do," Smith told a reporter when asked how she was occupying the last few hours before the president arrived in Skowhegan. "What any woman would do, obviously, is to look after the little things."

The reporter, Larry Colton, said that Smith would have little to do in her house, describing the senator's one-story home as "ready at all times for guests, even such a distinguished personage as the Chief Executive." Colton gave credit to the senator's housekeeper, Mrs. Agnes Staples.

Before the president arrived, Senator Smith's administrative assistant, William C. Lewis, Jr., of Skowhegan, put on gloves and work clothes and touched up the landscaping around the senator's house.

"Although Ike has visited more pretentious homes, it's safe to say he has been a guest at none more charming," wrote Colton. "He'll like the spacious lawn, and it's almost a certainty that he'll want to putt a few times on the tiny nine-hole golf course which runs around the house. Because he'll spend most of his time outdoors Monday, weather permitting, he's sure to appreciate the breathtaking view as the lawn slopes away to the north bank of the Kennebec River, with Skowhegan looming to the east and the beautiful valley toward Norridgewock to the east."

Throughout the day, crowds of curious people started to line the streets to Sen. Smith's house. As the presidential procession arrived at Smith's home after their visit to the fair, the crowd greeted the president and the senator with cheers of "Hi, Ike!" and "Where Is Our Senator Chase!" filling the warm summer air.

Reporter Bud Leavitt said that Eisenhower was at his gracious best during his two-hour stop at Smith's home. After the meal, the president walked up to outdoor chefs Ken Pray of Boothbay and Phil Goggins of Boothbay Harbor and congratulated each for their excellent job of preparing the dinner of lobsters and clams.

"How do you fellows do this all alone?" Eisenhower asked.

The president, himself a talented cook, particularly in the field of charcoaled steaks, listened intently while Goggins explained how it was done.

"Well done, boys, well done," Eisenhower replied.

Senator Smith also hosted a special reception given to members of the press, radio, television, and newsreel group covering the president's Northern New England Maine trip at a field at her home.

The president and Senator Smith casually walked to the field, where the ninety reporters in attendance were digging into their cookout of lobster and steamed clams. Eisenhower and Smith each borrowed a camera from the photographers and switched roles with the press corps. Eisenhower photographed the reporters going through the food line and had a word for those he recognized. One Washington reporter asked Smith for a second lobster.

"Gracious sakes, isn't there enough lobsters?" Smith replied.

"Now don't you worry about him," Eisenhower interjected. "He's very capable of getting his share, I know."

After the reception at Senator Smith's, on the way to Dow Field in Bangor, the presidential party drove through Newport, where flags lined Main Street, which had been emptied of cars. School children were asked to carry signs that read "We Like Ike." One banner read "Ike's Our Pick in '56."

In Pittsfield, a large welcome sign had been placed early in the day at the entrance to town. Members of the American Legion met at their post home on Manson Street at 6:30 p.m. The VFW assembled at the corner of Forest and Central Street. Members of the Boy Scouts met at Hathorn Park. The marching line assembled at the park at 6:45 p.m. and proceeded down Park Street to Main Street, where the band stood at the entrance to Hunnewell Avenue between the Lancey House and the A&P store.

Four units of the Pittsfield Fire Department were stationed along Central Street. The civil defense team and the Pittsfield Police Department handled traffic and parking. The streets of Pittsfield were lined with members of that town's service organizations, waving flags of greeting for the president's drive-through at 7:30 that evening. The Pittsfield Community Band was uniformed in its green and grey trimmed with gold braid. They were joined by the Boy Scouts, Girl Scouts, Cub Scouts, and Brownies, all in full attire. Overhead could be seen yards of bunting, welcome posters, and huge portraits of President Eisenhower.

A crowd of an estimated 2,500 people greeted President Eisenhower as he drove through their town. Eisenhower had his driver slow down as he passed through so that he could wave to them all.

One Associated Press reporter told Leavitt that the reception at Pittsfield was the best he had seen: "I was amazed to see such a crowd of people, young and old alike. I have been on this trip for the past six days. The public reception at Pittsfield for my money was the finest display in six days."

President Eisenhower was making his way to Dow Field in Bangor for his flight back to Washington. Dow officials had spent the weekend making final preparations for President Eisenhower's arrival. This would be the first visit to Dow by a president, as well as the first visit by the entire Maine congressional delegation and the Maine governor. The president was expected at 8:25 Monday evening.

The Union Street gates of the base were opened at 5:00 p.m. VIPs were to use the Hammond Street gate but were to be there well in advance of the president's arrival. Parking was ample. Two hundred air police assisted the base provost marshal with the parking of cars and directing the crowd. The 195th Army Band of the Maine National Guard was to play a concert at Dow AFB that night from seven to eight o'clock. Local station W-TWO was to televise the president's visit, along with various radio stations.

The president's quaint Maine fishing trip quickly took on an international flair when Secretary of State Dulles arrived at Dow for an urgent conference with the president during the return flight from Maine to Washington, DC. The president and Dulles had originally planned to meet when the president was back in the nation's capital later that evening. Hagerty told reporters that the change in plan did not mean the situation was an emergency. By this time, Russia had expressed regret and had offered to pay part of the damages for the shot-down jet.

"But they have not offered all that we consider appropriate under the circumstances," Dulles told reporters.

When Dulles arrived at Dow, while waiting for the president's arrival, he almost immediately went into the Dow Officers' Club for a Maine lobster dinner.

The president arrived at the Hammond Street gate of Dow Field at exactly 8:20 p.m. The Loring Air Force Band from Limestone gave the military honors of four ruffles and flourishes and then played the National Anthem. President Eisenhower was greeted by Lieutenant William Delaney of Washington, DC, who escorted him to the ramp on the flight line. Eisenhower was greeted by a group of people selected from the Third Congressional District and by base officials. He then reviewed the honor flight of twenty men.

The president was introduced at the speaker's stand by Senator Smith. Curtis M. Hutchins, on behalf of the Bangor Chamber of Commerce, presented the president with an eight-foot Thomas fly rod. There was a gift also for Mrs. Eisenhower, a luncheon set of mirror-black and seagull-gray pottery made in Blue Hill.

President Eisenhower was dressed in a brown suit and brown necktie with a light brown fedora. In a brief address to the crowd, he said he had enjoyed himself during his visit and wished that he could personally tell each person he had seen, "it is so good to see you—another American."

The president expressed gratitude for the work that went into his visit to Dow and for the chance to thank the Maine people for hosting him. He said he had made a lot of friends, had a lot of fun, and had found people very hospitable. He said he had met some salmon and trout, and a few midges. President Eisenhower praised Maine's natural beauty.

"I have had some vacation and done some work—now I must go back to work," Eisenhower said. He remarked that Secretary Dulles had flown to Bangor just to ensure the president did get back to work.

"He seemed in a happy holiday mood as he greeted the welcoming committee, but there was no question but that he was anxious to be on his way," wrote the *News*.

A rumor started circulating after the visit that President Eisenhower had refused the lobster at Senator Smith's in favor of a steak. Senator Smith was quick to refute the rumor, saying the president reported his lobster was "the sweetest one I've ever tasted" Smith said the president told her there are only two food items he passes up—parsnips and shrimp. The president's doctor told the *Washington Post* and *Times Herald* that he advised Eisenhower to forgo shell food for a time.

"He had a perfectly delightful trip," said Hagerty at Skowhegan. "The fishing was grand, and the folks of New England made a tremendous impression on the president."

Reporter Bud Leavitt reported after the visit that Western Union reported a file of two million words on the president's six-day tour through the New England states of Maine, New Hampshire, and Vermont. Another reporter estimated that the word *Par-Mar-Chee-Nee* was mispronounced by traveling radio reporters at least 3,500 different ways. One network commentator kept referring to the lake as "'Parmesan'—a man, no doubt addicted to spaghetti with ample shakings of grated cheese."

The *Bangor Daily News* ran an editorial aimed at the president. They still looked for help with President Roosevelt's Quoddy Village project, twenty years after President Franklin D. Roosevelt had visited Eastport.

Don't Forget Us, Mr. President

Mr. President:

You will be leaving Maine this evening after a brief visit. We hope you had a good time. We'd like you to come again sometime and stay longer and see more.

There are a few things we would like to say about your presidency before you board your plane at Dow Air force Base.

First, your calming influence in Washington has been refreshing. And more important to the welfare of the nation than most people realize. Little good could be accomplished in the turbulent sort of atmosphere that existed when you took office. A steady hand is needed at the wheel when the ship of state is in stormy waters. You have provided it.

We're glad you agreed to sit down at the big four "summit" conference next month. Some Americans are apprehensive about this meeting. They remember Yalta and other sessions with the Communists and fear the U.S. will again be hornswoggled. We don't think you'll let this happen. We believe you have by now sized up the Kremlin crowd pretty well.

We're confident you'll stand firm for western principles of human freedom and a peace based on mutual good-will, which is the only kind of peach worth its name. We don't believe you'll "buy" any tricky kremlin offers—such as granting a concession to the communists in return for the release of American captives, who should be freed anyway.

We feel that you are handling affairs well on the home front. The country is enjoying its first sound prosperity since some time before the 1929 crash. Prosperous periods between then and now have been by-products of shooting wars. Your middle-of-the-road, hands-off philosophy has helped to steady our whole economy. It lets private enterprise show what it can do when not treated as a political whipping boy.

Before closing, we want to put in a few urgent words for our fine State of Maine. You haven't been in politics long so you may not realize that Maine is frequently slighted in Washington. Our delegation in Congress does not always get all the help is should get, not even from the Republican party. Maine's traditional Republicanism is taken for granted. But the voters are getting restless. Democrat Muskie's election to the governorship showed that.

The people of Maine, you understand, have no "gimme" attitude about federal funds. We pride ourselves on being as self-reliant as possible in these complicated and burdensome times. But even our moderate and reasonable requests encounter obstacles in Washington.

Consider the plight of Washington county. If ever an area in the nation needed federal assistance, this is it. Yet the dreary struggle goes on to get $3,000,000 for a survey of the Quoddy tidal power project. The federal government has poured out billions for the TVA (Tennessee Valley Authority) and other power projects. It has helped France finance the very sort of tidal project proposed at Quoddy. Surely it can pay some attention, therefore, to the troubles of Washington county, where the sturdy citizens are waging a dogged struggle to share the prosperity enjoyed elsewhere in the nation.

There are other things, like the repeated and needless fights we have to put up to get federal funds for our fine Maritime Academy, but going into all of them would take too long. We just ask you and others of your administration to remember the State of Maine, not so much for its Republicanism as for the fact that the citizens are loyal, solid Americans—none better anywhere—who are entitled to fair consideration in Washington.

Wishing you a second term, we remain Sincerely yours, *The Bangor Daily News.*

On July 24, 1955, a month after his first visit to Maine, President and Mrs. Eisenhower landed early Sunday morning at Dow Field in Bangor; the first American stop on the president's trip home from a summit conference in Geneva, Switzerland.

The Big Four summit was a meeting of four nations; the United States, the Soviet Union, Britain, and France, to help ease international tensions.

President Eisenhower arrived in Maine at 6:37 a.m. aboard the presidential plane *Columbine III*, which was refueling at Dow Air Force Base after flying non-stop from Prestwick, Scotland, after the conference ended. A brisk tailwind helped the plane—piloted by Lieutenant Colonel William Draper—land sixteen minutes ahead of schedule. The stopover took exactly thirty minutes.

Lieutenant Colonel Draper had chosen Dow Field over other locations as the refueling spot specifically because he remembered the quick and efficient service that had been provided by that base during the president's last visit the month before. The refueling had taken only a few minutes, but the plane was not scheduled to leave for a half hour, so the president spent his time talking with base officials.

President Eisenhower emerged from the plane wearing a gray tweed jacket with brown trousers, white shirt, and a plain brown tie. Shortly afterwards, Mrs. Eisenhower opened the door, looked outside quickly, saw the photographers, and ducked back in the plane.

"So, in typical feminine fashion, she shunned the cameras," wrote *Bangor Daily News* reporter Robert Taylor.

Murray Snyder, the acting presidential press secretary, said the first lady had expected only Air Force officials, not reporters. The president's son, Major John Eisenhower, was also aboard.

President Eisenhower was greeted by base commander Colonel Robert F. Layton and Colonel Orie O. Schurter, commander of the Air Refueling Wing. A handful of newsmen and base officials were the only people to get near the plane. Eisenhower was hatless and carried a pair of horn-rimmed glasses, folding them up and putting them in the jacket pocket. President Eisenhower refused to comment on the recent Big Four conference in Geneva. Taylor said the president looked tired.

Arrangements had been made by Dow officials for a big breakfast for the presidential party, but the officials were informed the Eisenhowers had eaten on the plane about an hour before they landed. They did request fresh drinking water and coffee, and four gallons of cold water and two gallons of hot coffee were quickly carried aboard the presidential plane.

As the hour of 7:00 a.m. approached, Colonel Draper caught the president's attention and motioned toward the plane.

"Are we ready to go, Bill?" the president shouted to Draper in response, over the loudness of the jet's engines.

Halfway up the plane's steps President Eisenhower stopped and gave a final wave to the awaiting photographers.

The president had been hoping for a Sunday newspaper during his stopover. A frantic search was made, but none could be found. A car was dispatched into Bangor, but the plane had left before the car returned.

The following evening, July 25, from the Oval Office in the White House, Eisenhower held a press conference, described as a chatty, informal talk to the nation. President Eisenhower declared that the Geneva Conference brought a sharpened realization by the world that the United States would go to any length, consistent with our concepts of decency, justice and right, to obtain peace.

Fourteen years after his visit to Maine, upon President Eisenhower's death, he was eulogized Richard Nixon, who had served as Eisenhower's vice president:

> Some men are considered great because they lead great armies, or they lead powerful nations. For eight years now, Dwight Eisenhower has neither commanded an army nor led a nation; and yet he remained through his final days the world's most admired and respected man, truly the first citizen of the world.

John F. Kennedy

The assassination came with sharpened personal meaning.

—Dr. Lloyd Elliott, President of the University of Maine at Orono

John F. Kennedy was forty-five years old when he visited Maine for the first time as president of the United States. Born in the neighboring state of Massachusetts, Kennedy was one of eight children born to Joseph P. Kennedy, Sr., and Rose Fitzgerald.

Kennedy graduated from Harvard and was in the Navy during World War II, where he commanded a series of PT boats in the Pacific theater, almost costing Kennedy his life. Kennedy went on to defeat Richard M. Nixon and became the youngest person elected to the office of the president of the United States.

John F. Kennedy's first visit to Maine as president was going to be private, a weekend of rest and relaxation on a small island off the coast, at the summer home of Gene Turney, a former world heavyweight boxing champion. President Kennedy's visit coincided with the annual Summer Festival that opened on Thursday, August 9, at the Brunswick Air Station, which featured the Navy Blue Angels. Because of the extra visitors for the air show, along with the tourist population on an August weekend in Maine, a crowd of a hundred thousand was expected to be on hand at the air base for President Kennedy's arrival.

At first there was some confusion regarding whether Maine's Governor John H. Reed, a Republican, would be in Brunswick to greet the Democratic president. At first Governor Reed said he would not be greeting President Kennedy, a Democrat, but later it was announced that the governor had changed his mind. However, as of Thursday,

August 9, the day before Kennedy's arrival in Maine, the governor had not received an invitation from the White House to the event. Officials at the Brunswick Naval Air Station said that a seat was being planned on the speaker's platform for Governor Reed but that they understood the governor would absent himself from the event.

Painting crews had been busy all week at the Brunswick Naval Air Station. The base's regular painting schedule had been advanced by months to take care of the maintenance now. Lawns were mowed, shrubs trimmed, trees planted, holes patched, and additional flagpoles erected. A base spokesman said that sailors had volunteered their own time to get things shipshape for their fellow Navy man's visit.

"Considering that the President won't be here more than ten or fifteen minutes, we're doing a heck of a lot of work," said one serviceman.

The Maine National Guard had spent the morning of President Kennedy's arrival performing a dry run of their twenty-one gun salute, and they spent the rest of the day polishing the howitzers and other equipment. A detachment of sailors, Waves, airmen, and Marines practiced forming the honor guard through which President Kennedy would pass as he stepped from his plane.

On Friday, the gates to the base were opened to the public at 1:00 p.m., and visitors steadily arrived, despite the rain.

"The weatherman will be a very uncooperative fellow for most of the weekend," wrote Maxwell Wiesenthal, staff reporter for the *Portland Evening Express.*

Extensive security measures had been taken all during the week before Kennedy's arrival. The area surrounding the speaker's platform was roped off with oil drum barriers placed strategically, with ropes strung through them, and at every twenty feet stood a uniformed member of the Navy. Other sailors, along with the state police and the Secret Service were all over the base, all prepared for any eventuality.

Due to rain and fog, it was thought Kennedy might arrive by Navy ship at Bath Iron Works (BIW). Plans were made for that contingency. A special dock had been erected at BIW, and top state officials were at the yard until after Kennedy arrived and left the air base. Bath Police Chief Robert E. Wagner had placed his department in a state of alert and was prepared to block off traffic completely in the area surrounding

Route 1 and BIW had the president boarded a navy boat instead of an airplane. Several scores of people waited in the rain at BIW just in case President Kennedy should arrive there.

Shortly before six o'clock, however, the rain slackened and the skies brightened just a little, and the president was able to land at Brunswick Naval Air Station. The chartered plane carrying forty Washington newsmen had barely landed when the presidential 707 came in. The newsmen had to run to the press area near the speaker's platform to be there before the opening of the ceremony.

As President Kennedy's plane touched down at Brunswick Naval Air Station, there began a twenty-one gun salute, with National Guard units firing seven rounds each from three 55mm cannons.

The First Naval District Band played ruffles and flourishes and "Hail to the Chief" as President Kennedy stepped off the plane, and then they played "The Marine's Hymn" as he inspected the Marine Corps Honor Guard.

Senator Edmund Muskie, a fellow navy man, served as President Kennedy's host for the weekend. He introduced the president to those on the speakers' platform, including Governor Reed, a fellow PT boat captain.

Governor Reed extended a cordial welcome to President Kennedy and presented him with a wooden carving as the state's official welcoming gift. The work of Richard Steele of Rockport, the carving depicted a bearded sailor wearing a sou'wester hat and a pea coat, standing behind a ship's wheel, his hands gripping the spokes. Governor Reed had picked the gift out himself.

Having arrived by navy plane just ahead of Kennedy, Senator Smith also greeted the president. Kennedy addressed his fellow New Englanders:

> The New England states lack some of the great natural resources which have brought prosperity to other sections of the country. But the great asset which we have is the ability, independence, and commitment of our people themselves, and I believe that these states which helped found our country will occupy a position of leadership.

Kennedy talked about former president Franklin Delano Roosevelt. The bridge named for Roosevelt, which links Maine and Campobello Island in Canada, was dedicated five days later. He thanked the people of Maine for his welcome to the state.

"I want to express my warm appreciation to you for coming out in the rain," said Kennedy in his brief speech. "I'm glad to be in Maine, whether it rains or shines. I'm privileged to be with you."

Kennedy was dressed in a gray suit and wore no hat or topcoat. He stopped and talked with navy officers, inspected the Marine Honor Guard, and walked up to the crowd twice and shook hands with several of those who had braved the rain for the occasion. He appeared to enjoy his visit to the air station and seemed in no great hurry to continue on with his trip.

The unscheduled shaking of hands in the crowd caused a few hectic, scurrying moments for Secret Service agents.

"The last time Mr. Kennedy came to Maine he was a presidential candidate. Yesterday he came as the head of the nation. As a candidate he left his associates to shake hands and greet well-wishers gathered to cheer him. This time, as President, he left his associates to shake hands and greet well-wishers who cheered him perhaps more lustily. Secret Service men must have ulcers," wrote the *Evening Express.*

President Kennedy then entered a waiting white convertible for the short trip from the speaker's platform to the helicopter, riding slowly by the crowd, sitting up high in the car with Senator Muskie, waving his return greetings to the thousands of spectators.

About forty-five minutes after President Kennedy's arrival in Maine, three Marine helicopters were taking the presidential party to John's Island for the weekend.

"There were no outward incidents whatever to mar the visit," wrote the *Bath Daily Times.* "The crowd was warm and enthusiastic in its welcome for the President, and orderly at all times."

The *Portland Evening Express* was more succinct: "A red carpet was rolled out, the band played "Hail To The Chief," and the 21-gun salute had the area reverberating like Merrymeeting Bay on the opening day of the duck season."

Moored off Mouse Island was the *Guardian*, a super-secret converted PT boat that handled communications for the president while he was boating. Off Johns Island, the president's home for the weekend, a lobsterman said the "water is literally crawling" with strange watercraft.

Boat rental agencies had been doing good business in the Boothbay Harbor and Pemaquid region. Most of the rentals were to government agencies and some to press associations and national TV news photographers.

On Saturday morning Kennedy was up early and boarded the *Guardian* for the short trip from Johns Island to Burnt Island, where the yawl *Manitou*, a sixty-two-foot coast guard training vessel, was moored. Senator Muskie accompanied the president, along with a party of Kennedy's old friends.

Press Secretary Pierre Salinger, wearing a blue sweater and gray-green corduroy trousers, had accompanied the president on his trip. At 9:00 a.m., from the porch of the Village Inn, Salinger announced the names of the reporters who would accompany the president on a sail, in a separate boat.

"Salinger appears much thinner than jowly photos make him seem" wrote the *Evening Express.*

Eleven reporters followed Kennedy on his sailing trip, while the others checked out the town, relaxing, taking short boat trips, or just enjoying the scenery. *The Portland Evening Express* ran an editorial on Saturday aimed at the Kennedy family:

All in all, it was a rather wet Friday for the Kennedy family.

President Kennedy, as everyone knows, came to Maine seeking a weekend respite from Washington, political and international heat, and had to hang around in a drizzle making a speech and shaking hands.

Over in Italy, as everyone knows, Jackie and Caroline Kennedy are taking a vacation. We're not quite sure what it's from, but they're vacationing. Jackie is an expert on water skis, but the water was so rough in Salerno Bay that she was dumped unceremoniously into the Mediterranean. She tried again with Caroline but they both were popped into the briny.

Anyhow, the Kennedy family takes such things in stride. The President charmed the spectators in Maine. Jackie and Caroline were serenaded by an Italian band and the first Lady stopped to shake hands with the leader while fourteen-year old Caroline clapped gleefully.

Better diplomacy than that you just can't get.

President Kennedy spent some time on Saturday evening working on a speech he was expected to give on live national television Monday night.

Word went around the area that President Kennedy was expected to attend church services the following day, it was just not known which church he would attend. People agreed that there were three possibilities: Kennedy had been invited to attend St. Patrick's Catholic Church in Damariscotta, described as the oldest catholic structure in New England. The Brunswick Naval Air Station was being made ready in case the president chose to attend services there. The newsmen figured Kennedy would attend the Church of our Lady, Queen of Peace.

Saturday night the news media were given a clambake with live music. Chicago newsman Philip W. Dodd suffered back injuries and a forehead gash when he fell about ten feet on slippery rocks at the event. On Monday morning Dodd was taken from Boothbay Harbor's St. Andrews Hospital to Brunswick by ambulance. He was flown back to Washington on the presidential plane.

On Sunday, President Kennedy would ultimately attend services at the Church of our Lady, Queen of Peace in Boothbay Harbor, with the Rev. Francis Mannette at the pulpit. Kennedy was unexpectedly accompanied to church by his sister, Pat Lawford. Originally Mrs. Lawford had flown to Hollywood to attend the funeral of Kennedy family friend Marilyn Monroe, only to find that she was not among the thirty-one invited guests. Instead she flew to Boothbay Harbor to join her brother.

Boothbay Harbor was in a festive mood that weekend. The town was already full with its regular summer visitors, and, with the navy air show and the visit of the president, it was expected that more than forty-five thousand people would be there over the weekend. All town flags were flying for the weekend. Huge banners had been hung over roads leading into the town. More than fifty welcome placards had been distributed to storekeepers. Stores and shops were adorned with signs reading "The Boothbay Harbor Region welcomes President Kennedy and staff."

Saul Hayes, owner of the local movie theater, used his marquee to erect a message saying, "Mr. President, welcome to Boothbay Harbor."

After church, in the afternoon President Kennedy and his party again boarded the coast guard ship *Manitou* for more sailing. The presidential party was aboard the *Manitou* for more than two hours before Kennedy had to cut his recreation short and return to work on the speech that he would deliver on national television the following evening. It was believed that the president would ask for a cut in taxes in that speech.

On Sunday evening, Kennedy issued a statement congratulating the Soviet Union for its latest feat in launching two cosmonauts, in separate vehicles, into the Earth's orbit. The president also announced that he had appointed Francis Henry Russell of Turner, Maine, as ambassador to Tunisia. Russell was a career foreign service officer.

On Monday morning, with the weekend over, President Kennedy arrived back at the Brunswick Naval Air Station by helicopter at 9:58 a.m. The presidential jet left the runway twelve minutes later.

The president was wearing a blue pinstriped suit and sporting just a hint of a windburn across the bridge of his nose.

"He had fine sailing weather and an excellent weekend," wrote the *Evening Express.*

It had been expected that senators Muskie and Smith would travel back to Washington with the president, but instead Muskie flew in the morning from Brunswick to Lubec for the ceremonies involving the new Franklin D. Roosevelt bridge. Senator Smith had flown back to Washington from Brunswick the day before.

Before leaving, Kennedy shook hands with state police detectives and Secret Service agents who accompanied him throughout the weekend. The president did take a few minutes to talk briefly with Maine newsmen about development of the natural resources of Maine.

Kennedy listed three areas "which deserve our vigorous support," technological development, development of the St. John River, and development of the Allagash area. Kennedy said the St. John River was almost wholly undeveloped and was possibly the most important river in this part of the United States. The president said his Secretary of the Interior, Stewart Udall, had a survey underway and would make recommends "for action we can take in cooperation with the state government and with Canada for helping development of Maine's natural resources."

"We have only one suggestion for Mr. Kennedy if he returns," wrote the *Evening Express*. "Bring Jackie."

All the local Maine television stations carried President Kennedy's address that evening.

For what was planned to be a relatively quick, simple visit, John F. Kennedy's second trip to Maine as president was running into several complications just days before the president was due to arrive.

Kennedy was in the middle of campaigning for another four years in the White House. The idea for President Kennedy to visit the University of Maine was that of Senator Edmund Muskie. Kennedy agreed to give a speech and receive an honorary degree at the University of Maine at Orono. The whole event would take place during UMO's Homecoming Weekend.

There had been a snag with an invitation for Senator Smith to participate in Saturday's program. The popular Smith was expected to run for president the following year, on the Republican ticket, potentially facing Kennedy in the election. The senator had contended earlier in the week that she had not received an invitation to the convocation at which Kennedy would speak.

Dr. Lloyd Elliott, President of the University of Maine at Orono, said that he understood Senator Smith was expected to accompany Kennedy to Maine in the presidential plane. Dr. Elliott explained that the university had been advised by the White House that all details in connection with the issuance of invitations to the Maine delegation would be handled by the White House.

There was a flurry of telegrams among all parties. Dr. Elliott said the series of telegrams were "to clarify a misunderstanding" about the

Saturday program. The university sent a telegram to Senator Smith, extending a personal invitation to the ceremony.

Dr. Elliot wrote:

> Let me report that no invitations have been issued to any members of the Maine congressional delegation except those extended by the White House. The invitation to accompany President Kennedy, issued by the White House, was interpreted by me to include the university convocation, and in anticipation of attendance we have secured caps and gowns for you, Senator Muskie, and congressmen McIntire and Tupper. Since your interpretation of the White House invitation apparently differs from mine, I am hereby extending this special invitation to you to be a platform guest at the convocation. A similar invitation is being sent today to other members of the Maine delegation lest they too feel the university has been remiss.

Senator Smith responded that she would "accept with pleasure" the special invitation sent to her by Dr. Elliott. This cleared the way for all the congressional delegation to participate in the ceremonies. An aide to Smith said the senator was not miffed, but did consider it a roundabout method, despite the high level, to receive an invitation by way of the White House.

President Kennedy also faced political sniping in advance of his visit. The *Bangor Daily News* printed a series of editorials attacking administration's policies. On Wednesday, that newspaper ran an editorial taking the Kennedy administration to task on trade policies that were hurting the state's textile, shoe, farming, and fishing industries:

> Upon taking office, you urged your fellow Americans not to ask their country what it could do for them but what they could do for their country. Well, the employers and employees of Maine are making solid sacrifices for their country because of your administration's trade policies. They will make more if the state—already without railroad passenger service—is given worse rather than

better air service. After three years, it is time the country did a little thinking about what it can and should do for the state of Maine.

Sincerely yours, the *Bangor Daily News*

On the day of Kennedy's visit, the same newspaper printed an editorial regarding Quoddy Village and President Kennedy's plan to fly over the project site after his visit to Orono.

Flyover Is Best

Have just finished reading about the President's proposed fly over of the "Quoddy Site.

That's the safest way for him to view Eastport. That way he can't see the deserted houses of people forced to leave their homes and all they hold dear in order to earn a living. He'll miss the downtown district with its blank store windows of shops forced to close or burnt out.

He'll not have to see the faces of people who didn't earn $400 this year in the sardine factories or those who managed to by "factory hopping," that is by working in two factories at the same time.

Let our city manager or councilors or any of the city fathers say Eastport isn't dying. It isn't it's dead. It died a little bit with the closing of each shoe factory, sewing factory, fish processing plant, all hurt a little by foreign imports.

So "Good Luck" Mr. President on your flight. View the pretty sights and don't see the anxious, bitter and disgusted faces turned up to watch you fly over.

Political sniping over Kennedy's visit also came from others. State Republicans said Muskie's popularity was on the wane and that Kennedy's visit was a way to shore up Muskie in a challenging race for Muskie's Senate seat.

"It looks to me that the President considers this a good opportunity to present himself before a large Maine gathering to see what he can pick up for himself and Senator Muskie," said Miss Helen C. Mitchell, Houlton, one of two Maine members of the Republican National Committee.

"I wonder if he'd have come to Maine at all if Senator Muskie—the state's lone Democrat in Congress—wasn't coming up for re-election next year," said the *Bangor Daily News* in an editorial two days after Kennedy's visit.

There was an especially big snag the night before Kennedy's visit, when Old Town police received a bomb threat at 9:00 p.m. on Friday. Old Town Police Chief Otis LaBree said the bomb threat was received by a telephone operator and relayed to him while he was conferring on final security measures for the president's visit.

The phone call was traced to an area on South Fourth Street. Chief LaBree, accompanied by two Secret Service agents and state and local police, started a house-to-house check of the area. Other agents rushed to Alumni Field, where the bomb was reportedly set to go off twenty minutes after the threat.

According to newspaper reports, police interrogated forty-three people seeking to locate the caller before twenty-four-year-old Robert C. Cartier of Biddeford admitted to making the call. Cartier, a freshman Democratic state representative, was found at a house party at one of the homes. Cartier told authorities he made the call as a party prank, to break up a football rally being held at Alumni Field so that more guests would attend the house party. After Cartier's confession, the Secret Service made the decision not to cancel the president's visit.

During the week, elaborate security details had been worked out between Secret Service and campus security. Stephen Gould, chief of the campus security force, was in charge of a small army of law enforcement officers Saturday. Gould was the coordinator of all security measures except those involving the president's immediate person.

The special force was comprised of approximately 150 officers from the Maine State Police, the Penobscot County Sheriff's Office, Dow Air Force Base, campus police, and the police departments of Bangor, Brewer, Orono, and Old town.

Saturday was described as one of the most beautiful autumn days in history, a beautiful "Indian Summer" day.

President Kennedy arrived at Dow Air Base in Bangor at 10:34 a.m., along with Senators Smith and Muskie, and Maine Congressman Stanley Tupper. The president was wearing an oxford gray suit and medium blue tie and carrying a hat. An aide carried a London fog raincoat.

"The president is apparently allergic to hats, and one can well imagine that Mrs. Kennedy might have suggested a hat," wrote Nelle Penley, Women's Editor for the *Bangor Daily News*. Even at the UMO ceremony, Kennedy removed his mortar board before speaking.

Kennedy was greeted by an honor guard of twenty Air Force personnel at the air base. He chatted briefly with reporters.

"President Kennedy has charm of a high order, which struck people with whom he chatted Saturday following his landing at Dow AFB," wrote Penley. She noted that the president spent his brief time at the base talking to the dependent children of the base instead of the voters. As he approached those children, they let up a spontaneous "hurrah."

Technical Sergeant Robert MacMillan, a 1949 graduate of Bangor High School, served as a flight attendant on the presidential aircraft that carried President Kennedy to Bangor, and had been doing so for the past four years. His parents, Mrs. Katherine Andrews of Searsport and father, Clayton G. MacMillan of Sidney Street in Bangor, were at Dow to visit with their son while the plane waited for the return of its passengers.

Upon getting in the helicopter for UMO, Kennedy immediately reviewed the press kit that had been prepared. Guests at Dow watched the ceremonies at Orono on a television at the officer's club on the base. Over a hundred newspaper, wire service, radio, and television representatives were expected to be at the university's special convocation.

The ceremony in Orono was covered live by WABI television and broadcast by that station for the Maine Association of Broadcasters. All Maine TV stations and at least eighteen of the state's radio stations were in the cooperative hookup.

"Welcome, Mr. President" was the banner headline in the Saturday edition of the *Bangor Daily News*. "Where all Roads Lead Today" was an editorial cartoon in that day's edition of the paper. The cartoon showed a picture of JFK at the podium on the athletic fields at UMO. The paper also ran an editorial urging the people of Maine to turn out to greet their president:

> We hope Maine citizens will turn out in large numbers and give President Kennedy a warm welcome when he visits the University of Maine and receives an honorary degree today.
>
> The convocation is open to the public and barring a bad turn in the weather—which is not expected—the President should receive a hearty welcome. And not by dignitaries alone, but by the citizens.
>
> John F. Kennedy, along with being the Chief Executive of this great nation, is also leader of the free world in the struggle against communism. He is trying to cope with vast and critical problems. His responsibilities are almost beyond comprehension. Any man in his position can use an encouraging pat on the back. That's why we hope there will be an overflow turnout when the President comes to Orono this morning for a brief speech and to receive an honorary degree.
>
> The occasion is a single honor to the state. The state should do no less than honor him in turn, putting aside whatever political differences may exist. Let's show him some genuine Down East hospitality.

The gates to the university's athletic field were opened to the public at 9:00 a.m. and all seats were on a first-come, first-served basis. Some law enforcement officers were used to direct the thousands of cars arriving at the University of Maine at Orono campus. Early arrivals were parked at the ends of the campus and other cars closer to the field.

At 10:30 a.m. the various high school bands that had been invited to the ceremony began playing for the arriving spectators. They included the Orono High School Band, the Old Town High School Band, the Piscataquis Community High School Band at Guilford, the Bangor High School Band, and the Stearns High School Band.

"And undoubtedly never before had there been so many children on the university's athletic field. Fathers and mothers, probably tired and weary even before they reached the field because of long trips from home, carried babies in their arms and conveyed older tots in push carts and other types of small vehicles. Fathers carried small children on their backs and shoulders. And even the family dogs were brought along," wrote the *News*. "Everybody wanted to see and hear the President."

Steady applause greeted the president as he stepped from the helicopter and stopped briefly to don his gown and cap. The president walked toward the infield to the strains of "Hail to the Chief." A great roar went up from the crowd.

Kennedy was escorted to the speakers' platform by Dr. Elliott, who introduced Governor John H. Reed. The governor conveyed the official state welcome to President Kennedy and the members of the congressional delegation.

In introducing President John F. Kennedy, Dr. Elliot told the crowd that the University of Maine trustees had voted to confer the honorary degree to Kennedy "in recognition of what you are: The President of all the people of this land, the weak and the strong, the white and the colored, the rural and the urban, the rich and the poor, the young and the old."

A wide smile split Kennedy's face when Dr. Elliott told him that "henceforth, wherever you may travel around the world, and in whatever circles you may find yourself—in stately halls with titled diplomats or in the playroom with Caroline and John—it will be your solemn obligation to stand and sing whenever you hear the Maine 'Stein Song.'"

President Kennedy spoke to the crowd for twenty minutes. He talked about the need for a more exact understanding of the true correlation of force in the conduct of foreign affairs. Kennedy said the U.S. firmness during the last year's October missile crisis had changed Soviet-American relations, but it was too early to assume that the change was permanent.

"There are new rays of hope on the horizon, but we still live in the shadow of war," warned Kennedy.

An audience of fifteen thousand people watched with "obvious enjoyment" as the president spoke and received his honorary degree.

After the conferment of the degree to President Kennedy, the ceremony was closed with the singing of the Maine "Stein Song," "which the university's newest alumnus sang with commendable accuracy."

As the presidential party was leaving the speakers' platform, Senator Muskie noticed former campus president Dr. Arthur A. Hauck in the audience. Dr. Hauck had served for twenty-five years in that role. Senator Muskie quickly motioned for Dr. Hauck to approach the podium and shake Kennedy's hand, which he did. Dr. Hauck appeared obviously pleased and grateful at the gesture.

On the way back to the helicopter, Kennedy made an unexpected turn into the crowd to shake hands. Secret Service agents flocked to his side.

The temperature was in the low seventies. Several of the band members standing at attention were overcome by the heat and were treated at the infirmary.

The helicopter was delayed in leaving after the ceremony because Senator Smith was giving an interview to the *Bangor Daily News*. A presidential aide ran to the senator.

"Hurry up, Senator, we are ready to go," called the aide.

Muskie, Smith, and others accompanied the president on his fly-over of Quoddy Village after the Orono visit.

The headline in the November 21, 1963, edition of the *Bangor Daily News* was small and run-of-the-mill: "Kennedy, Johnson Start Texas Visit."

During the Texas visit, President Kennedy was scheduled to dedicate the Aerospace Medical Center in San Antonio, which was devoted to keeping men alive in space. Friday night there was to be an $100-a-plate dinner in Austin. The plan was for the presidential party to spend the night at Johnson's Texas ranch after the speech.

Instead, on Friday, November 22, President John F. Kennedy was met with a flurry of bullets as his motorcade made its way through the streets of Dallas. The Kennedy Era's age of innocence was over.

At one moment, a man alive, healthy, and smiling; a man waving to well-wishers as he rides with his wife in broad daylight along the street of an American city.

The next moment, a man felled by a bullet; inert and dying in his wife's lap as stunned witnesses gasped in disbelief.

Thus did death come yesterday to John Fitzgerald Kennedy at the prime of his life and of his brilliant political career—a good man, a good American, dedicated to serving his country in war and peace . . .

Unbelievable.

But it has to be believed; It happened. Hate brooded in a twisted mind—brooded and planned, and then pulled the trigger of the assassin's gun.

And so today, the nation mourns the loss of a good man, a good American—a man who risked his life in battle but lost it, ironically, in peace.

—*Bangor Daily News*

"Virtually every public political figure in our state—whether Republican or Democrat—expressed disbelief and horror at the act which took the life of the President," reported the *Bangor Daily News.*

Maine's Senator Margaret Chase Smith was expected to announce her candidacy for the White House in just a few days, a decision that could have put her in direct competition with President Kennedy.

Senator Smith had just returned to her office in the Washington, DC, senate building after having attended a committee hearing. Smith was eating her traditional luncheon of cottage cheese and peach salad when she heard that President Kennedy had been shot.

"I am deeply shocked," said Senator Smith, in tears. "I pray for his recovery. In the past weeks, we had become such very good friends—he was so generous to me,"

Senator Smith left her unfinished lunch on her desk. Having filmed a television show earlier in the day, Smith canceled all her remaining appointments for the day.

Senator Smith had planned to announce on December 5 her intentions to run in the presidential primaries. Lewis said the senator was unsure if she would keep the appointment. She later canceled it.

Senator Muskie was sitting in the Eastland Motor Hotel lobby in Portland when the news of the shooting came in.

Members of the New England Society of Editors had just finished luncheon in the same hotel when the news of the assassination attempt broke. Editors quickly lined up at telephones to call their papers. The convention, scheduled to continue through Saturday, was quickly canceled.

Visibly shaken, Senator Muskie went to the studios of WCSH-TV in the same building to watch newscasts. He was described as being visibly upset and on the verge of tears. Muskie said he was in "no mood" to continue his speaking engagement in Maine and would return to Washington immediately. At one point, while listening to the news, he wiped his eyes.

"[I]t's difficult to comprehend the motive of anyone who would do this to his country," said Muskie privately, but he made no public comment until he confirmed the news that President Kennedy had died:

"We have lost a great leader and I, a good friend. I am sure he would be the first to say that now is the time to pray for our country. It's never easy to accept a thing of this kind. We must all emphasize our dedication to our country."

Congressman Clifford McIntire, Maine Second District, was in Boston at the time of Kennedy's shooting. He was informed of Kennedy's death by an airline attaché as he prepared to leave for Maine. It was not until he arrived in Bangor that McIntire found out Johnson had been sworn in as president. Congressman McIntire made a statement at the Bangor International Airport during a stopover while en route to Presque Isle, calling it one of the saddest days.

"The loss of this great young leader of the free world has consequences beyond our momentary comprehension," said Congressman McIntire.

The congressman arrived in Presque Isle Friday night to participate in Saturday's scheduled dedication of the Northeastern Maine Vocational Institute in Presque Isle. The event was canceled. McIntire said he would return to Washington as soon as definite word of funeral arrangements had been made.

Congressman Stanley Tupper said, "[T]his is the most tragic circumstance since the assassination of Abraham Lincoln. Every person in this land who encouraged the vicious extremism that unleased this murderous assassin on President Kennedy and Governor Connally and every politician who has not raised his voice against the paranoids of the radical group are equally guilty."

In Augusta, Governor John Reed was visibly shocked. Flags throughout the state were quickly lowered to half-mast.

"Words are inadequate to express my shock and sorrow at the ruthless assassination of President Kennedy," said Governor Reed. "This is one of the most tragic moments in the history of our country. It is unbelievable that the President is gone. Maine has lost a great friend. The people of our state join with me in expressing our heartfelt sympathy to all members of his family."

Citizens in Augusta were stunned. At the State House, employees and department heads visited the newsroom to read the shocking bulletins as the tragedy unfolded. They stood in little groups about the offices and corridors, many with portable radios tuned in. Every face was grave, many were pale.

"An outrageous rape of our government," one official said in quiet anger.

Governor Reed sent a telegram to Mrs. Kennedy, expressing the "deepest sorrow at the tragic loss of your husband and our president. This nation has lost a great leader and its people a great friend. While I realize that words are inadequate at this sad time please accept our deepest personal sympathy and our condolences to your family."

Later Governor Reed sent a telegram to the newly sworn-in President Lyndon Johnson:

> The citizens of the State of Maine stand behind you in this tragic hour as we grieve for our fallen President. Fate has placed the destiny of our nation in your capable hands. I personally have great confidence in your leadership and pledge to you my loyal support as you assume the burdens of the presidency. May Almighty God be with you now and in the future.

Governor Reed proclaimed a thirty-day period of mourning throughout the state of Maine. He asked that all people suspend their usual activities on Monday during the funeral.

Whereas, the life of our beloved President of the United States of America has been untimely taken; and

Whereas, this profound tragedy has shocked and saddened the citizens of the State of Maine; and

Whereas, the State, Nation, and entire World have lost by death a great leader, distinguished statesman, and true patriot; and

Whereas, the citizens of the State of Maine wish to express publicly their overwhelming grief at the death of President John F. Kennedy, who in his direction of national affairs and deep and abiding faith in the underlying strength of this country, won their admiration and respect while he lived; and

Whereas, we wish to extend our deepest sympathy to his bereaved family and to acknowledge the will of the Almighty to call His faithful servants to greater service;

Now, therefore, I, John H. Reed, Governor of the State of Maine, do hereby proclaim a period of mourning in this State to continue for a period of thirty days from this date. As a tribute of respect to the memory of our fallen President, I order that flags on all state buildings be flown at half-staff during this period. I further request that on the occasion of the funeral of the President that the Citizens of Maine refrain from their accustomed pursuits and that this time be observed with deepest reverence and in prayer for our departed Chief of State and the future of the United States of America.

At the University of Maine at Orono, Dr. Elliott said, "The assassination came with sharpened personal meaning."

Throughout the state of Maine, statements were issued, plans were canceled. People were in shock. Below is a partial list of reactions throughout the state. The shorter list would have been what was not called off from Friday through Monday.

The Republican and Democratic state headquarters in Augusta and Lewiston were ordered closed.

Attorney Alton A. Lessard of Lewiston, former Democratic State Committee chair, was in Portland with Senator Muskie when he was informed of the president's death: "I am just shocked beyond expression and just cannot believe our President has been assassinated. President Kennedy was an exceptional gentleman with a tremendous personality, and his tragic death most certainly is a great loss not only to our country but the whole world."

"We have lost a great leader, and wonderful human being," said Democratic State Committee Chairman William D. Hathaway of Auburn, who would later serve in the United States Senate.

"In this sad hour the profound sympathy which goes out to the President's family knows no bound of party or station in life but is, I am sure, shared by every American," said David A. Nichols, Chairman of the Republican State Committee.

State Senate President Robert A. Marden, Republican of Waterville, said he spoke for other leaders of the Republican legislative majority in "expressing our shock and sadness at this loss, which transcends political lines."

Van Buren Democratic County Chair Elmer Violette said, "God help us. We hear about things like this happening in Africa, but can it happen here in the United States? Our country is supposed to be the most civilized in the world. That's the only thing I can say. God help us is all I can say. I'm crying. I'm incoherent. I'm awfully sorry."

"Like all American citizens, I am shocked and grieved at the death of the President. Partisan politics should be put aside when such a tragedy strikes," said Malcolm S. Stevenson, Chairman of the Republican City Committee of Bangor.

"President Kennedy's death is a tremendous shock to the nation, state and community. He certainly was a dynamic figure who had tremendous influence throughout the entire world," said Bangor City Manager Joseph R. Coupal.

Court sessions throughout the state were canceled. For Maine schools, the school day was coming to an end when the president died. An assembly of students was scheduled for 2:00 p.m. at Madison Memorial High School. Principal Alex Richard had been informed of the assassination attempt before the assembly began but delayed making an announcement until definite word was received that Kennedy was dead.

"I told them there was one announcement I had to make, as much as I regretted the necessity of it. They took the news in complete quiet. A television set was brought in and I told the students that they were welcome to stay, instead of returning to their classes if they wanted to. Many did stay to hear of later developments and walked around with bowed heads."

Students at Skowhegan High School were given the news over the school's public address system. Principal Maurice Noonan said, "I asked them to rise and give a silent prayer for one minute." Bangor High School Freshman Barbara Goode said on Friday, "It was so hard to believe. I felt just empty and couldn't believe it happened."

In Machias, the Machias High School senior play "Lock, Stock and Lipstick," was postponed. At Rockland, the second night of the annual senior class play planned Friday evening was postponed until the following Tuesday.

At South Portland, the state board of education chairman Bernal B. Allen announced that all public schools in the state would be closed during the school session when the president's funeral was held Monday.

A round-robin of basketball games scheduled by the Upper Kennebec Valley League at Bingham was canceled. A tournament in York County was postponed. At Thomaston, a game between Georges Valley High School and its alumni was called off. Other games canceled Friday included Addison at Cherryfield, Beals at Princeton, Jonesport at Harrington, Milbridge at Jonesboro, and Vanceboro at Woodland.

The University of Maine's varsity basketball squad had been en route to Boston Friday to play a scrimmage game with Massachusetts Institute of Technology, but State Police halted the bus carrying Coach Brian McCall and his team to notify them the game was canceled, and why.

The Sylvania plant in Waldoboro closed Friday afternoon shortly after receiving news of Kennedy's death, and remained closed Saturday. An employees' party scheduled for Saturday evening also was postponed.

A Rockland native was living in Dallas at the time of the assassination. E. Daniel Flanagan said in a telephone interview Friday evening, "You can't see a smile anywhere down here. The whole city is in a state of shock." Flanagan was a laboratory technician at the Dallas Diagnostic Laboratories and had seen the presidential motorcade pass by and had started back to work. "When they told me later that he had been shot, I couldn't believe it—I thought it was some kind of a joke."

Bells of Roman Catholic churches throughout the state tolled for ten minutes at 6:00 p.m.

Maine Council of Churches president Dr. Mervin M. Deems of Bangor issued the following statement:

> The people of this country have lost a devoted and courageous public servant. The free peoples of the world have lost a symbol of hope and strength. The good causes for which the late president stood are now become, more than ever before, the responsibility of the Congress and of us all. They must become our concern in a spirit of dedication. All people of good will grieve now, but also take heart and courageously press forward.

"President John F. Kennedy led America with wisdom, courage, honor and dignity. He will go down in history as one of the greatest American presidents. He was the Abraham Lincoln of the 20th Century," said Reverend John D. Protopapas, pastor of St. George's Greek Orthodox Church, Bangor.

"One hundred years after Lincoln, President Kennedy, with his Civil Rights Bill, was determined to complete the unfinished business of the Civil War. We do not know what motivated the man who assassinated the President, but this we do know, that President Kennedy and Abraham Lincoln shared the same faith. Our President was a man of deep faith, of indomitable courage, of a vision which was always prophetic," said Rabbi A. H. Freedman, spiritual leader of the Congregation Beth Israel, Bangor.

In Caribou, the United Baptist Church did not postpone its 100th birthday celebration. The event featured ladies in poke bonnets and lantern light on the tables in the church basement. Reverend Newall

Smith, the pastor of the church, did ask for a moment of silence in memory of the late president.

Reaction was coming in from people who had interacted with President Kennedy during his two visits to Maine in office. William Roper, caretaker of the Tunney Estate, where President Kennedy spent the weekend in 1962, was reached at South Bristol. "The only thing I can say is this is a terrible, terrible shock to me because he was one grand individual," said Roper. "I know it's an awful loss to everybody. That's all I can say."

Stanley Lyons of Presque Isle, president of the Maine Association of Broadcasters, recommended in a message to other broadcasters that commercial messages be eliminated until Saturday noon and on the day of the funeral. He requested "good taste in programming" and that music moods be "toned down in consideration of the tragedy." But he said the nation and state should "not be kept in a depressed mood by broadcasters over too lengthy a period."

On Saturday, November 23, the day after Kennedy's death, most events in Maine and across the country came to a halt. Meetings, sports events, and social activities were canceled or postponed out of respect and out of a feeling of disinterest in the ordinary during extraordinary times.

In Newburgh, the firemen's ball scheduled for Saturday evening at the Newburgh Elementary School was postponed until December. The Eastern Maine roundup of encampments of the IOOF, slated Saturday afternoon and evening at the Odd Fellows Hall in Lincoln, was canceled. A penny carnival slated for Saturday at the Owls Head Central School was postponed.

At Woodland, Paul Phelan, director of music in Woodland schools, announced that a band practice scheduled Saturday at Woodland High School had been canceled. The Starlite Theta Rho Club also canceled its planned installation of officers Saturday evening at the IOOF Hall in Woodland.

The meeting of Bangor Area Ski Patrol, scheduled for the Bangor House, was postponed until Tuesday evening. The Santa Claus Parade scheduled for downtown Bangor on November 30 was postponed for a future date after a unanimous vote of the Downtown Merchants

Bureau. The usual weekend colored comic paper would be omitted from the state's newspapers until Monday.

The Saturday edition of the *Bangor Daily News* featured a large picture of President Kennedy with one of the stanzas of the song "America":

> O beautiful, for heroes proved
> In liberating strife,
> Who more than self their country loved
> And mercy more than life
>
> America! America!
> God shed His grace on thee,
> And crown thy good with brotherhood
> From sea to shining sea.

The paper also printed an editorial cartoon with the caption "To You, From Failing Hands."

The feature showed a torch with Kennedy's name on it, the flame burning, with the words "Peace with freedom—justice for all."

With the underlying fear of Communism in the 1940s and 1950s, and not knowing exactly who was behind Kennedy's assassination, an editorial in the same paper the same day seemed to give a warning:

> "J. Edgar Hoover, chief of the Federal Bureau of Investigation, doesn't mince words—no double-talk, no euphemisms. He is blunt and to the point. As a result, you know just what he is talking about. He makes the picture clear."—Communists.

Marion Flood French, author of the *Bangor Daily News* column "Windows of The Times," wrote about Kennedy's spirit.

> Usually the view from our workday window includes the red and white stripes of our country's flag snapping crisply in the breeze. Today we see only the blue field and its stars as it hangs at half-staff. And everyone is aware that it honors not just the office but

the man. There is a phrase which describes men who merit this honor . . . "his spirit has more of the eagle."

His enthusiastic dedication belied every tired excuse we ever use to postpone meaningful living. We say our lives would be happier if we had wealth, yet his wealth could not assuage grief after grief which afflicted his vibrant family nor avoid the final disaster. We say we could achieve if we had our health and strength, yet it must, at times, have seemed for both him and his lovely wife, that the past few years were one long ambulance chase after another. He was never a stranger to physical pain; his strength had to be an inner one. We say if I were an intellectual, but he knew that intellect does not grow in an ivory tower. We say if my faith were different, but he knew true faith is bounded with love and compassion. We say he was just beginning to live. He knew you live every moment. You don't wait.

His spirit had more of the eagle.

The *Bangor Daily News* remembered President Kennedy's visit to UMO less than a month before:

But perhaps the most vivid recollection of John Fitzgerald Kennedy is the last one at least for most Maine people. That was the October visit at the university.

It was a short visit, but was only a month ago and those who were there will recall University President Lloyd Elliott telling Kennedy that the trustees had voted to confer the honorary degree on him in recognition of what you are: the President of all the people of this land—the weak and the strong, the white and the colored, the rural and the urban, the rich and the poor, the young and the old.

It was a proud moment and there are 15,000 people who, whenever the presidency is mentioned, will see Kennedy as he was then, standing in the sun at Alumni Memorial Athletic Field, a vital, forceful image of the President of the United States.

The *Bangor Daily News* reached out to State Police Commander Lieutenant Edward J. Doyle, who had headed state law enforcement officers during President Kennedy's visit less than a month before.

"I doubt if such a thing could have happened here," said Doyle.

The Secret Service insisted on heavy security and that's what we provided. There were virtually no buildings nearby where a sniper could have hidden himself with the exception of the field house, and I expect the Secret Service was aware of that fact. We had several meetings with the President's security staff as to how to provide maximum safety, and we even had to list the names of all officers at key points.

Doyle also noted that there were several emergency cars placed around the area in case there was an emergency, including two cars stationed on I-95, where the interstate runs by the airport runway, to make sure no one with a rifle caused trouble when the presidential plane made its landing in Bangor.

During the UMO visit, when President Kennedy unexpectedly went to shake hands in the crowd, Doyle quoted a Secret Service agent as saying, "[W]here the hang is he going now?"

Doyle said President Kennedy went out of his way to speak to him, greeting Doyle during the walk to the podium at UMO.

"Nice to see you, lieutenant," said Kennedy.

"Nice to see you, Mr. President," replied Doyle.

Doyle had also been a driver when then–Senator Kennedy was campaigning in Maine in the late fifties. Due to inclement weather, Doyle was to have driven Kennedy from Auburn to Rockland, where he was to make a speech. At the last minute, the plane was able to fly, so Doyle's visit with Kennedy was cut short.

"He was a nice man to speak with," said Doyle. "When he spoke to you, you felt as though you were talking with someone familiar."

"It was obvious that Lt. Doyle felt as if he had lost a friend," wrote the *News*.

Bud Leavitt, noted *Bangor Daily News* outdoor reporter, talked to local gun expert William Morrison. Morrison said the gun shown by police as the one that was used to kill Kennedy looked like a cheap rifle, likely an Italian-made Carcano. Morrison said that type of gun was being imported into the United States by the Golden State Arms Co. of Pasadena, California, and was valued at $20 and that the rifle appeared to have a $9.75 telescope. The Italians stopped manufacturing the 7.35 rifle in 1938, when they discovered that the gun was not providing "enough stopping power," said Morrison.

Morrison said the gun, if fired at a 45-degree angle, had an extreme range of two miles. He called the rifle the "cheapest quality of equipment" with unreliable accuracy beyond two hundred yards.

"The gun is commonly used in the State of Maine," said Morrison. "They may be purchased out of magazines anywhere in the country."

In Washington on Sunday, Governor Reed attended a memorial service at Calvary Baptist Church and heard a eulogy by the Reverend Dr. Clarence Carmford, former pastor of a Lewiston church.

Maine's pioneer radio preacher devoted his farewell on the airwaves Sunday to a brief service of prayer and meditation in memory of President Kennedy.

The Reverend Howard O. Hough retired at age sixty-five as pastor of the First Radio Parish of American, which he had founded thirty-eight years previously. His sermon was broadcast by WCSH television.

When it seemed as though things could not get worse for the nation, regular television programming was interrupted on Sunday for another bulletin, another shooting, another killing, on live television. This time it was Lee Harvey Oswald, the man accused of killing the president.

Maine jurists deplored Sunday the shooting of Oswald.

"A judge, just like the common man on the street, doesn't like to see this sort of a thing. I should hope that we're covered by the rule of law instead of the law of man. No man has the right to take a life," said Abraham M. Rudman, Bangor superior court justice.

"Oswald should have been given every opportunity to stand trial and defend himself. Two wrongs do not make a right. After all, we still as a nation of laws and we all should let the law take its course," said Judge of Probate George M. Davis of Skowhegan.

The *Bangor Daily News* summed up the mood of the region on Sunday in a piece called "As A City Wept:"

> Bangor wept Sunday.
>
> Quietly, reverently, the people of the Penobscot River Valley went to their churches to pray.
>
> Grief was silent.
>
> Skies were clear and an eight-knot northwest wind, an off-shore breeze on the Coast of Maine, portended a good voyage for sailor Jack Kennedy, president of the United States of America.
>
> Colorful holiday displays in downtown store windows gave way to somber but appropriate tributes to a fallen leader.
>
> Streets of this old lumbering town were deserted. The few who were aboard seemed to walk in funeral cadence and the soft Maine speech was muffled.
>
> Neighbor met neighbor. A nod, an understanding.
>
> This was the way of Bangor Sunday, November 24, 1963.

Monday, the day of President Kennedy's funeral, had been declared a national day of mourning by President Lyndon Baines Johnson.

"Today's sorrow must be borne," wrote the *Bangor Daily News*. "Life must go on. The struggle must go on. The burden is made lighter by the outpouring of sympathy that has streamed into the nation's capital from the plain, good people of the world. They have faith in America. This strengthens the faith of Americans in themselves. And so now to the sad task of saying farewell to John Fitzgerald Kennedy— whose dedicated service to his country was cut short by an assassin's bullet."

Along with the coverage of Kennedy's upcoming funeral in the Monday edition of the *Bangor Daily News*, was an 8 x 11 picture of Oswald being shot.

The advertising departments of the state's newspapers had a problem. Newspaper ads at a time like this seemed in bad taste. However, many companies had a standard space in the newspapers already laid out. Something had to fill the void. Companies instead filled those spaces with tributes to the slain president.

New England Telephone and Telegraph Company, in an 8 x 11 ad, wrote a tribute:

"All who love freedom will mourn his death."—Lyndon B. Johnson

> John Fitzgerald Kennedy
> 35th President
> of the United States

The freedom of men he fought for, the dignity of men he stood for, the future of men he prayed for—these ideals he has left with us to carry forward. With his courage, let us take heart and proceed to the task.

Other advertisements were respectful, and almost gave a glimmer of hope for the end of the national nightmare:

All Red and White and Shop n' Save stores closed from 11 to 2.
Watch for our big Thanksgiving ad in tomorrow's news, Tue., Nov. 26.

There was confusion over which businesses should close on Monday for the observance of the National Day of Mourning by the new president.

Governor Reed had recommended that state-chartered banks close on Monday out of respect to Kennedy. He sent his recommendations from Washington, where he had gone to attend the president's funeral.

"The law requires more than a recommendation—it requires a proclamation," responded Halsey Smith, president of the Casco Bank and Trust Co. "The law is a peculiar one and we feel obligated to follow it."

State Banking Commissioner David O. Garceau, with whom Governor Reed had consulted before making his recommendation, disagreed. He said he did not know of any law that required that state banks remain open. Garceau recommended that bank presidents put the question to their respective boards of directors.

A compromise was reached. Limited service was announced by state banks: "One or more of our key people will be on duty to provide emergency services during regular banking hours as required by state and national laws. Our other officers and employees have been excused. We are hopeful that our bank customers will join us in attending services of their choice in solemn memory of our beloved President," wrote the Bangor Savings Bank and six others in an advertisement in various state newspapers.

All national banks would be closed throughout the day. Certain essential businesses such as food and drug stores and essential distributing concerns were to remain open. Many of those places, however, were planning to be closed from 11:00 to 2:00.

There was no mail route delivery except for special delivery. But outgoing mail would be collected, and incoming mail would be distributed to post office boxes.

All county offices were closed with the exception of the sheriff's office. No court sessions were held.

Willard L. Babb, chairman of the Calais City Council, proclaimed a period of mourning of thirty days and requested that all places of business within the Calais area remain closed Monday until noon. Stores, schools, and businesses in Jonesport and Calais were remaining closed the entire day. In Machias, it was decided that stores would be closed from noon until 2:00 p.m. after a paper was circulated to merchants on Saturday asking their opinion on the matter.

At Bath Iron Works, production went on as usual, with a brief memorial service at noon. In Portland, the city's biggest employer, the S. D. Warren Company, advised employees it would be impossible to shut down its Westbrook paper-making machines for such a short period. It did say, however, that anyone who had not been able to pay his final tribute to Kennedy could be excused between 11:00 and 2:00.

The Maine State Ferry suspended operations from 11:00 to 2:00. The planned dedication of the new Georges Valley School in Thomaston was postponed for two weeks. In Searsport, there was a suspension of the three-act play "Take Your Medicine," sponsored by the Searsport High School Dramatics club, until Tuesday, when it would be performed in the Memorial Gymnasium.

In Portland, in the business district, Monday was like a Sunday, only quieter. Almost every store and office was closed. Few cars moved on Congress Street, normally jammed bumper to bumper on a Monday.

While President Kennedy was being laid to rest in Washington, DC, that Monday, many special church services were held across Maine. Some Roman Catholic churches had special children's services. An overflow crowd of four hundred attended an interfaith service in the morning at the Episcopal Church of St. Mary the Virgin in Falmouth Foreside. The Machias Valley Baptist Church joined with the Machias Methodist and Congregational churches in a joint memorial service Monday at 12:00 noon, held at the Machias Congregational Church.

"Churches will be open—as will the hearts of the people," wrote the *News*.

In Washington, just before the funeral, Senator Smith, who was known for wearing a rose every day on her blouse, laid a red rose atop a back-row desk in the Senate Chamber, a sign of respect for her departed Senate colleague.

Senator Smith placed the rose during a brief ceremonial session preceding Kennedy's funeral. It was an unscheduled gesture. The Senate Democratic leader was giving a short eulogy during the ceremony. Smith entered through the main doors at the rear of the chamber. She stopped at the last row of desks, just inside the doors, took the rose from a miniature vase pinned to the lapel of her coat, and put it on the second desk to her left. This was the desk occupied by Kennedy when he was a Massachusetts senator.

A twenty-one gun salute was fired from the Maine State House in Augusta at same time that taps was being sounded over Kennedy's body in Arlington National Cemetery. That salute was fired by the same National Guard unit that had saluted Kennedy's arrival in Brunswick in August 1962.

At the time of the funeral, in newsrooms across the state, the news wires went silent in the middle of the funeral report at the same time as the playing of taps. The *Bangor Daily News* described how it was in their office in a story with the headline, "Thoughtful Time":

The usually busy editorial room of the *Bangor Daily News* was quiet Monday afternoon. No phones rang and few people were concerned with local events. The overshadowing national sorrow took precedence here, too.

Main Street in any town in Maine Monday afternoon was a mournful place on a mournful day. During the hours from noon to after 3 p.m., few persons could be seen; stores were closed and darkened; coffee shops featured the vacant stool; and nowhere was there a smile. Time seemed to stand still.

Main Street at Presque Isle was flag-lined but cold and empty. Two small boys whistled to hear their echoes bounce back from the forlorn buildings and kicked a stick ahead of them as they walked.

At the Northeastland Hotel a small group of customers sat huddled over cups of coffee in near silence.

At Houlton, it looked like Sunday—but even more so. In Market Square, businesses and offices were closed. The streets were empty except for a few teenagers, a few strollers, and the usual one or two who gather under the protective eye of a building at Kendall and Bangor streets.

In the midcoastal region, the flapping of American flags at half-staff in a stiff breeze was seen on the main streets of Rockland, Camden, and Thomaston. Traffic was virtually non-existent. Display window lights in the stores were turned off.

Skowhegan's main street, Water Street, was unusually quiet. Most stores were darkened, and those that remained open did not display window lights. The parking lot never contained more than two dozen vehicles at a time.

Those who had to work gathered before television sets and watched the funeral cortege of the late president. No one spoke. Everyone seemed immersed in his own thoughts and didn't have the heart to inject them upon others.

Some of the eyes were moist. Others seemed to stare without seeing. A bowed head could be noted as prayers were recited at the cathedral and at Arlington National Cemetery.

But the impressiveness was in the quiet. There were no words—none were needed.

And outside, as the last notes of taps sounded from Arlington, Main Street in Maine was bathed in a warm orange glow as the sun peeked out from behind a scattering of clouds.

When the ceremonies at the cemetery concluded, the employees filed from the room and went quietly back to work.

And as the sun sank lower, members of a local American Legion post began to gather up the flags which lined Main Street, rolled them carefully and took them away.

Main Street in Machias was almost a reverent scene in midday. There were no persons visible and shops were quiet until after 3 p.m., when a trickle of people slowly picked their way along the sidewalks.

Rockland began to stir slowly at nightfall as some citizens made their way toward special church services, but few vehicles were seen on the streets. A few persons wandered along the main stem, stopping occasionally to speak briefly and then hurrying away. There was only one topic of conversation and the subject matter as limited by choice.

Bangor Daily News writer Virginia London gave a summary of what that Monday was like:

Bangor was hushed Monday. Little traffic moved, streets remained empty, and people were in their homes throughout the day. For most it had been a strange weekend with necessary tasks interrupted by thoughts turning back to Friday's shocking event.

By Sunday, a quiet thoughtfulness prevailed as the city paid its respect in church services and eulogies. All were touched with a feeling of near unbelief of the known facts and, with the rest of the country, remained in the grip of national tragedy.

Monday, Bangor and the nation paid final tribute to its leader, the late President John F. Kennedy. Many went to their respective churches at some time during the day to pray. They went to pray for the President whose untimely death had so affected the nation and the world, and to pray for his family and loved ones. They went to pray for President Lyndon B. Johnson, who has taken up the nation's leadership. They went, also, because in times of stress it is the way of America's people to seek God.

Others remained at home, following the late president's family through their final hours of church services and military honors, selecting this as their way of paying homage to a fallen leader.

By nightfall Monday, as continuity of government in Washington was picked up by President Johnson and capitol officials; so, in Bangor, the mood of the city lightened. Cars began to move in greater numbers as some sought entertainment for relief from the strain of the troubled weekend; and the quiet of the city was broken.

By Tuesday, the state was trying to get back to normal. Thanksgiving was in just a few days, Christmas in just a few weeks. Governor Reed returned to Maine Tuesday morning, arriving at the Augusta State Airport. The governor was traveling home aboard a Maine Air National Guard plane, along with General Edwin Heywood, the state's adjutant general, and Reginald B. Bowden, the governor's press secretary. Governor Reed called the funeral rites "a profoundly moving experience."

Governor Reed said he was particularly impressed by "the remarkably dignified composure which Mrs. Kennedy maintained throughout the long ordeal." Reed said the crowds in the nation's capital were extremely respectful and silent throughout the series of solemn, moving ceremonies on Saturday and Sunday. He noted the impressive number of world leaders who gathered to pay their final respects to Kennedy.

Governor Reed had a chance to meet the new president during his time in Washington for Kennedy's funeral. Reed said President Johnson asked the thirty-five governors at the meeting to support important measures in the field of education, civil rights, and taxation, which he promised to outline later. The meeting was on Monday night.

"I was very much impressed by President Johnson's sincere request for unity and his desire to work closely with all the governors and both parties. His grasp of world problems is very apparent."

Representative Stanley R. Tupper, a Republican, called for a moratorium on partisan politics for at least the remainder of the year "to demonstrate the unity of our people behind President Johnson."

"It is vital that the world know that President Johnson is the president of all the people just as his predecessor was and that our government is built upon something more mortal than man," said Tupper.

Maine-born Thomas S. Estes, U.S. ambassador to Upper Volta, bade farewell to President Kennedy only the day before his assassination. One half hour before Kennedy flew to Texas on Thursday, Estes paid a call to the president.

Estes had been at his Limington, Maine, home on Friday when he heard of the assassination and immediately flew to Washington. On Tuesday, Estes paused in Portland and told a reporter he had assured President Johnson of Volta's friendship toward the United States.

Estes said he had been prepared to turn in his resignation if that had been what President Johnson had wanted, but that Johnson "was ahead of all of us. He asked us not to resign." Estes said that Johnson asked of the ambassadors "to carry out a policy of continuity—and I'm on my way back to do just that."

It was announced on Tuesday that Senator Smith had canceled all speaking, television, radio, and newspaper commitments for the remainder of the year. She would later announce her candidacy for the White House, and she would lose badly in the primaries.

After reopening on Tuesday, bookstores in Portland found they had a run on books by and about Kennedy, including *Profiles in Courage, PT 109,* and *To Turn the Tide.*

The University of Maine John F. Kennedy Memorial Scholarship Fund was created on Sunday, before the president had been laid to rest. The money would be used to assist worthy students.

Bud Leavitt in his "Outdoors" column in the *Bangor Daily News,* discussed the issue of gun control:

> You know something, firearms fans?
>
> The recent dreadful and inexcusable Dallas doings have put a new pressure to disarm the citizen.

Already pulpits have carried forth words that firearms legislation is an absolute necessity if we are to avoid the heartache of the last 72 hours. You know this all adds up to a mouthful of politics and high-sounding oratory—emotion, without fact . . . yet, the little things like stealing a man's limit of game contribute to the decay of pride and something called sportsmanship in the field.

Never has the time been more apt to reflect—with a promise to lean more strongly in the direction of decency, fairness, and sportsmanship.

Bangor Daily News reporter Lorin Arnold said that Kennedy had hoped for a return visit to Maine, in particular to see the Passamaquoddy Tidal Power Project from the ground. Some White House staff members traveling with President Kennedy the previous month gave assurances to Maine state officials that Kennedy would return next year to make a ground tour of the Passamaquoddy region. Kennedy was also reportedly planning on visiting the president Franklin D. Roosevelt summer home at Campobello, which he had never seen.

Lyndon B. Johnson

I guess we were remembering things in Dallas, too.

—Unnamed official from Porteous, Mitchell & Braun,
a leading Portland department store at the time

P resident Lyndon Baines Johnson visited the State of Maine less than a year after President Kennedy's assassination, during a re-election campaign to keep the office he had inherited.

Donald E. Nicoll, coordinator of President Johnson's visit, said he expected more than fifteen thousand people to attend Johnson's rally in Portland. Nicoll said he had been getting calls from places as far away as Eastport and St. Francis on the Quebec border from people interested in attending.

On September 26, state and county Democratic officials started placing official signs along the Portland motorcade route that read "LBJ Motorcade Route. Monday Sept. 28, 5 p.m."

Clark Nelly, Portland Trade Board manager, said that all downtown stores would close at 5:00 p.m. so that store personnel would have a chance to see President Johnson.

The Secret Service seemed to be on trial by the Maine public during this visit. The Warren Commission report on President Kennedy's assassination had just been released, and it had been critical of the Secret Service's handling of security details for Kennedy's Texas visit. The commission discovered that some Secret Service agents had been found to have stayed out until nearly 3:00 a.m. the morning of Kennedy's assassination.

The week before the president's visit, two Secret Service agents had paid a quiet visit to the Maine Medical Center to make sure that all of their varied facilities would be immediately available should the president need them.

The agents informed the hospital of Johnson's blood type and instructed them to have plenty of it on hand.

The Secret Service agents also checked the names and qualifications of key hospital personnel, including the senior medical and surgical residents, and asked that these people be available during the president's visit.

They went over the emergency equipment in the hospital's emergency department and asked that all equipment be tested before the president's arrival in Portland. They also made sure the hospital's staff would be ready to go into action promptly and smoothly in the event of a mass casualty situation.

"They were very polite, but very firm," said Edward J. McGeachey, the assistant director of Maine Medical Center.

The Secret Service advance team scoured the city. They had checked out the owners of the buildings along the three-and-a-half miles of the presidential motorcade. Photographers in helicopters took pictures of every section of the city days before the president's arrival. The city of Portland provided maps to the agents.

An order went out that there were to be no open windows along the motorcade route. Citizens were warned to stay away from their windows. Most people did not observe the latter rule, but where Secret Service agents did see the noncompliance, they addressed it, with demands.

An official for Porteous, Mitchell & Braun, a Portland department store, said he had complied with the request even though other stores did not.

"I guess we were remembering things in Dallas, too," said the official.

Two Marine helicopters hovered overhead on the day of President Johnson's visit, scouring rooftops for snipers. Aboard one of the helicopters was a team of paramedics, ready to be landed or even to parachute to the ground should the president need them.

In the Fore River, near the airport, a forty-foot Coast Guard boat patrolled back and forth, prepared to assist if the plane carrying President Johnson should have to land in the water.

From City Hall Plaza, one could see uniformed police atop all the buildings of the area, including one man in the clock tower of city hall. The Secret Service was augmented by Maine State Police and Cumberland County Sheriff's Office personnel. There were also police in civilian clothes. They all wore a dime-sized metal tab on the lapel of their coat to distinguish them to each other.

During the visit, two girls opened a fire escape door on the second floor of the Masonic Building to get a better view of Johnson. In seconds three agents were pointing at the door and motioning to a man in a window to check it out. The man did, the girls disappeared, and the agents left when the door slammed shut.

Mike Jordan, a driver for the Portland Coach Company, was standing in front of Portland City Hall, waiting for the president to arrive. Because the president was delayed, and because of the chilly conditions, Jordan put his small camera in his coat pocket and then his hands in his pants pockets. His actions looked suspicious to a Secret Service agent, who frisked the man twice.

"It don't even pay to be a good Democrat," Jordan would quip to people who kidded him about the story.

Security even scrutinized the man who delivered the yellow roses that were to be presented to Mrs. Johnson upon her arrival. They cleared Portland City Hall of all but authorized personnel by 4:30 p.m.

Local television stations undertook the most ambitious local operation in its history—telecasting Johnson's visit.

WGAN-TV had a camera mounted on the roof of the airport administration building to televise Johnson's arrival. WCSH-TV had two cameras focused on the motorcade from a vantage point at the Congress Square Hotel, and WGAN-TV had two cameras pointed from the fourth-floor window of the Gannett Building toward City Hall Plaza for the speech. WMTW-TV joined WCSH and WGAN in carrying the entire proceedings.

All local and network programs were canceled between 6:30 and 8:35 p.m. by all three stations. The stations rejoined the networks until the motorcade returned to the airport, when they televised the president's departure. Television rating services estimated that 150,000 homes viewed programs over the three local stations between 6:30 and 8:30 p.m. on a Monday evening.

Downtown Portland streets were lined with flags. Welcome signs dotted store windows. A holiday atmosphere seemed to pervade the city in anticipation of the President Johnson's arrival. Delegations from Aroostook, Washington, and Penobscot counties had arrived in Portland the night before, and caravans from other sections of the state drove into the city early in the afternoon. Ten busloads came from Lewiston. One-hundred-and-ten students from Buckfield arrived in school buses.

The Veterans of World War I Band played at the airport. Eleven bands played along the route, their location determined by lot. The Deering High School Band played at city hall; the Portland High Band played at Monument Square; the South Portland High Band played at Congress and Brown streets; the Westbrook High Band played in front of Porteous, Mitchell, and Braun; the Biddeford High Band played in front of the Strand Theater; the St. Louis High Band played in front of the Portlander; the Lewiston High Band played at Congress and Temple streets; the Edward Little High band played at Longfellow Square; the Brunswick High Band played in front of J. E. Palmer's; the Harold T. Andres Post Band played at Free and Congress streets; and the South Portland VFW Band played in front of the Army Recruiting Office on Congress Street.

Governor Reed had come to Portland from Augusta to extend the state's official greetings to the president. He had planned to return to Augusta as soon as the presidential motorcade left, but the persuasive President Johnson had different ideas.

"[T]he president said I wouldn't interfere and that there would be no Democratic politics discussed if I went along," said Reed. "Still, I stood back, but the President got into his limousine and then he asked where I was."

The president came for Reed.

"I walked with him, arms locked, to the car," Reed said.

President Johnson was driven from the airport to Portland City Hall, along with Maine's Congressional Delegation. Reed said the ride to City Hall Plaza was unforgettable. The motorcade stopped twice before it left the airport parking area, to spontaneous screams and cheers from the crowd that thrilled the president

The motorcade made about eight stops between the airport and city hall, and the cars and buses following the president banged together several times. The motorcade stopped at Waldo and Congress streets, the Westgate Shopping Center, the Union Station Shopping Center, Bramhall Square, and three stops between Congress Street and Monument Square.

"The car stopped seven or eight times before we got to the city at all, and each time the President seemed more thrilled by it all," said Governor Reed. "I'm sure he was moved by the warmth of Maine people for their President,"

The frequent, unexpected stops in a motorcade that was supposed to keep moving caused a few fender-benders.

"Another photographer and I were sitting on the trunk of a car when one unexpected stop came," said a photographer assigned to cover the visit. "The fellow with me just pulled his feet up high when the bumpers crashed together. He probably would have lost his feet if he hadn't acted when he did. It's a wonder no one was hurt."

When the president arrived at the plaza, he wanted to meet the people, touch them, shake their hands. As he pressed into the crowd, Secret Service agents fought to surround him. Each time they did, President Johnson would break free again.

After the president finally walked up to the speaker's platform, a wall of security men and police was thrown against the crowd to keep it from following him. The crowd had broken through double rows of barricade horses to get as close as they did.

On the steps of city hall, President Johnson was greeted by City Council Chairman J. Weston Walch. Mrs. Walch presented the bouquet of yellow roses to Mrs. Johnson on behalf of the city. Mr. Walsh introduced Sen. Muskie, who introduced the president. President Johnson addressed the crowd.

"I have come to the forest city of Portland—in the great state of Maine—to talk to you about the future of America," Johnson said. "Nature has blessed Maine with a beauty unmatched in all the world. But the Lord's greatest gift to Maine is the quality of its people. The people of Maine have given America tradition of thrift, of industry, of independence, and of courage in the face of adversity."

Johnson praised Senators Smith and Muskie to the Portland crowd, saying they had helped build a prosperous America. "We are not going to turn it over to extreme and reckless men who would not hesitate to shatter all that has been so carefully built over so many years."

The crowd that turned out at city hall in Portland was estimated to be one of the biggest in Portland's history. Democrats quickly said it was an indication that Maine would vote Democrat in November. Republicans attributed the turnout to the office, not the man.

When he left, the president went through city hall and left by the Chestnut Street exit. As his car pulled away at the end of the visit, one Secret Service agent let out a small smile.

"That's that," said the agent, "I hope he gets to Manchester all right."

Mrs. Johnson donated the yellow roses to the Maine Medical Center, asking that the bouquet be given later to a little girl at "the hospital on the hill. Give them to a child old enough to enjoy them."

Joyce Enman, eleven years old, had watched the president's visit on a portable television set in Room 280 of Maine Medical Center. Joyce said she could not believe her eyes when the roses were delivered to her.

The daughter of Mrs. and Mrs. Charles Enman of Parris Street, Joyce was a sixth grader at Sacred Hearts School. She had been in the hospital for a hip-pinning and was expected to be on crutches for an indefinite period of time after being released.

President Johnson had been almost two hours late in arriving to Portland. The president's tardiness was good news for restaurants and bad news for retail stores along the motorcade route from Portland Municipal Airport to City Hall Plaza. Local restaurants did a thriving business, some running out of food to serve. Retail stores, on the other hand, did very little business after late afternoon crowds began forming along the motorcade route. Most stores closed from 5:00 to 6:15 p.m., as had been planned, though some smaller ones waited until the president actually landed at the airport before closing up shop. Because of the delay, some stores closed for the night, and some stuck to the original plan and reopened at 6:15 p.m. but did very little business. Linwood S. Cross of Cross Jewelers could tell by watching the television that the president would be late.

"When the motorcade left the airport, we closed up for the night."

The restaurants in Monument Square appeared to be the busiest, with one establishment hiring extra help for the evening.

"The coffee shop did a rushing business," said Alfred Dane, manager of Sears, Roebuck in Portland. "It was cleaned out of hot dogs. The parking lot was full but not of shoppers. Quite a few people came in the store for warmth and watched the proceedings on the television sets scattered throughout the store."

George Bress of George's Delicatessen, near Monument Square, said, "We have a seating capacity of about ninety and two hundred people walked in at supper time. We didn't have enough help to serve them all, couldn't make coffee fast enough and ran out of our specialty, rye bread, several times. People were happy and understanding for the most part," said Bress.

John Mayo of Your Host in Congress Square said that hot chocolate had been popular on the cold late afternoon in September. "We were extremely busy and ran out of several things. We hadn't anticipated such busines."

Bars in Portland stopped serving alcohol at 4:30 p.m. The Sportsman's Grille near Union Station reported losing money for that reason but said more families came in to eat supper.

At the Airport Restaurant, the line of customers extended all the way across the lobby to the Northeast Airlines counter.

"We ran out of everything and stocked up twice," said a restaurant spokesman. "We were busy when Goldwater was here, but it was nothing like yesterday."

Clark Nelly, manager of the Retail Trade Board of the Greater Portland Chamber of Commerce, said there had been no discussion about stores possibly staying open later another night to make up for the loss of sales.

"Portland put on a tremendous demonstration last night for the President of the United States," wrote the *Portland Press Herald*.

It was a splendid show, colorful with political posters and placards, bands and bugle corps, capped by political oratory. It took
on an eerie quality as the growing crowds waited patiently in
the dusk and floodlights were placed around City Hall. Many
Portlanders will remember that picture of that spot of bright
color at the platform standing out above the dark concourse of
close-packed bodies—the red, white, and blue bunting; Jane
Muskie in a green suit, Ladybird Johnson in a red suit, holding a
bouquet of yellow roses.

But above all else—above the pictures of a president standing on the hood of a car, boldly, even recklessly, reaching out to
grasp anonymous hands—the memory that will remain is that
of twenty thousand persons packed into the plaza and surrounding streets, and thousands more thronging Congress Street just
to catch a glimpse of the president as he went by. Plenty of effort
by the Democratic organization went into the preparation of this
welcome. But no amount of party effort could have turned out so
huge a crowd. The turnout of people regardless of politics was a
spontaneous thing.

Portland Evening Express photographers Donald Johnson and William Curran called the crowd that turned out "the greatest thing" they
had ever seen. They said the crowd in Portland during VJ Day was
nothing compared to the LBJ crowd. They said it was practically impossible to move.

After the president left, local and state police officials assigned to
protect Johnson drew a long sign of relief when the president's plane
left the runway. They marveled that no one was seriously injured in the
surging crowds that greeted Johnson at the airport and lined the motorcade route to city hall.

"All our prior plans simply went out the window from the moment
the president stepped from the plane and ran to the fence at the Airport to shake hands with the throngs," said Bangor Detective Captain
Edward M. Kochian, who traveled in the lead car with Secret Service
personnel. He said they were horrified when they saw the size and
enthusiasm of the crowd.

The president's insistence on the motorcade stopping for impromptu speeches along the route where large crowds had gathered caused concern for security personnel.

"Every time the motorcade stopped for one of those impromptu speeches, the crowds surged in from the side jamming the persons in front against the sides of the automobile." Kochian said the crowds for VJ and VE day during World War II were small in comparison. He said even a visit by Charles Lindbergh, an international hero, caused no problems compared to Johnson's frequent motorcade stops.

Every time someone fainted, a state trooper and men from the rescue squad rushed into the crowd to help. The Secret Service agents watched the crowd with a sharp eye lest the commotion cover something else.

Six people were casualties of Johnson's visit and were taken to Maine Medical Center for emergency treatment by police. Five of the six fainted and were released after treatment. The sixth, a fifty-four-year-old man, complained of chest pains in Longfellow Square and was admitted to the hospital.

Mrs. Mary Bertalan of Congress Street lost her handbag between Temple Street and Hub Furniture when the president went through. Mrs. Elton Howell lost her wristwatch. She was making a retreat with her two children because of the rush and lost the watch. She felt it go but dared not to try to retrieve it. It had been a gift from her husband.

A V-neck sweater was found at the scene after the crowd left. It was believed to be hand-knit. A woman had seen an eight-year-old boy drop it, but he was unable to pick it up because he was being forced along by the crowd.

Portland Public Works cleaned up the city the next day. The cleanup took twelve hours, and the debris was about five times the normal collection. Among items recovered were two handbags, a canvas school bag, and a woman's red shoe.

President Johnson's second visit to Maine was part of a whirlwind speech-making trip through five states, to conclude with a boat trip along the Maine coast from Portland to Campobello Island in New

Brunswick for talks with Canadian Prime Minister Lester Pearson. Johnson said the visit was nonpolitical.

Brunswick Naval Air Station was opened to the public beginning at two o'clock on the day of the visit. Base officials were preparing for a record crowd. The five thousand people that showed up to greet President Johnson were enthusiastic, despite the president being an hour behind schedule.

President Johnson arrived aboard the presidential jet. As he exited the aircraft, he was greeted by the Maine Congressional delegation. C. Warren Ring, chairman of the Brunswick board of selectmen, presented the president with a slate ashtray.

The president then turned in one direction, and his wife Lady Bird and daughter Lynda in another, to greet the crowd and shake hands.

Five minutes later the presidential entourage entered their limousines, which had been flown in earlier, and headed toward Lewiston. Traffic at the air station was not allowed to move for ten minutes before the president's arrival and after his departure.

Two hundred Marines and sailors were on duty as security guards while the president was there. Many could be seen on the roofs of buildings. A helicopter hovered overhead while the president was at the base. Officials at Brunswick Naval Air Station said the visit went off smoothly.

The entourage drove to Cook's Corner and turned onto the new highway, following Route 201. Outside of the Brunswick Dairy Queen was a large sign welcoming the president to the city. The motorcade stopped and an ice cream cone was ordered for President Johnson. When the USS *Lyndon Johnson* was set to be christened in April 2019, about sixty members of the ship's crew indulged in a frozen treat from the same Dairy Queen in honor of Johnson. The Dairy Queen now has a plaque that reads "L.B.J. Ate Here."

John N. Cole of Brunswick, who was part of the Bipartisan Alliance for Peace in Vietnam, said his group absolutely never considered any demonstration against the president. Cole said he welcomed the president's visit and the opportunity it afforded the people of Maine to get a firsthand report on Johnson's policies.

"Maine people are well-mannered and generally courteous to visitors, regardless of how we may feel about their political views," said Cole.

"President Johnson's entire journey through Maine was marked by friendliness," wrote one Maine newspaper. "Although he had met with signs protesting his policy in Vietnam elsewhere on his New England jaunt, he saw no such signs in Maine."

Gerald Ford, the current House Majority Leader, was in Bar Harbor at the time of President Johnson's visit.

A crowd estimated to number twenty-five thousand people was waiting to greet Johnson and hear him speak at what would later be named the John F. Kennedy Memorial Park in Lewiston.

President Johnson stood at the park in a Victorian bandstand with Governor Reed, Senator Smith, and Congressman Tupper, all Republicans. This seemed to be a Johnson strategy, having prominent Republicans accompany him on his visits to the Northern New England states.

"We haven't been talking party matters, we've been talking people matters," Johnson said in his speech from the bandstand.

The presidential party then motored from Lewiston to Portland.

"We like your beautiful Maine, we like the people, we come here whenever we can," the president shouted through a bullhorn to a crowd of four thousand at the Maine State Pier in Portland.

Mrs. Johnson took the bullhorn and said she was looking forward to a Maine lobster dinner. Daughter Lynda said she was exhausted. "I'm afraid I'm just not young enough to keep up with them," she said of her parents.

The presidential party went aboard the USS *Northampton* for an overnight cruise to Campobello Island, where President Johnson met with Canadian Prime Minister Lester Pearson.

Richard M. Nixon

He heard it all right. If there was one dissident in a crowd of ten thousand, he'd hear it. But he'd never let on.

—veteran member of the national press corps
to Bob Taylor of the *Bangor Daily News*

R ichard Milhous Nixon was fifty-eight years old when he first visited the state of Maine as president of the United States.

Nixon was born in California and was a veteran of World War II. He served as vice president under President Dwight D. Eisenhower. President Nixon ended American involvement in Vietnam, and he was the only president to resign from office.

Senator Margaret Chase Smith announced the visit of President Richard M. Nixon on Wednesday, August 4, two days before the president and his family arrived. The visit was to be a personal vacation weekend for the Nixon family.

Over the same weekend, in New Hampshire, Congressman Paul McCloskey opened his presidential campaign headquarters in Concord. McCloskey, who was from New Hampshire, was challenging Nixon in the GOP primary. Other presidential hopefuls were also to be in New Hampshire that weekend, including Maine's Senator Muskie, regarded by many political experts as the leading man for the Democratic nomination. President Nixon stopped in Nashua before flying to Bangor.

This was not Nixon's first visit to Maine. In 1960 he stopped at Bangor in a torrential downpour. A significantly large crowd turned out to hear him as he campaigned, and lost, against John F. Kennedy. Nixon addressed the Aroostook County Republican GOP Rally at the State

Teachers College in Presque Isle in 1964. In 1966 Nixon addressed a GOP gathering in Waterville. At the Waterville Armory, Nixon vowed then to press LBJ for the answers to what Nixon called "the Vietnam question."

Maine Governor Kenneth M. Curtis encouraged civic, service, veterans, youth, and senior citizen groups who wished to be represented in the presidential welcoming party to contact the governor's office. He announced there would be no charge for parking at the Bangor International Airport during the visit.

"I'm delighted that President Nixon is coming to our state," said Governor Curtis. "We definitely want a large crowd out at the airport. The larger the crowd, the better the chances that President Nixon will briefly address the crowd."

Flyers and posters were distributed throughout the midsection of the state Thursday, the day before the visit, by a Republican committee hastily organized Wednesday. "Give our President a warm Down East welcome," the flyers and posters said. The Welcoming Committee was headed by Representative Theodore S. Curtis, Jr., of Orono.

"The President's visit is an honor to our state, and we want to give him a real Down East welcome," Curtis told the press at a briefing.

Bangor Director of Development Edward G. McKeon was in charge of making arrangements at local motels for the president's advance team and press entourage. The Regency Room at the Twin City Motel in Brewer was turned into a press headquarters for the 120 national reporters traveling with the president. Press briefings were held there.

Nine phones were installed at Bangor International Airport for the reporters. One clerk at the Northeast Airlines desk reported that she had received many calls asking which flight the Nixons were taking to Maine.

Throughout Thursday night and Friday morning the police and Secret Service were busy investigating suspicious persons in the Bangor area. Many automobiles were said to have been stopped and checked out.

After the announcement of Nixon's visit, *Bangor Daily News* reporter Ken Buckley interviewed Mrs. Gerry Gartley of Greenville.

Her son, Lieutenant Mark Gartley, also of Greenville, was a Navy flyer who had been shot down over Vietnam.

Mrs. Gartley said the president and his advisor, Henry Kissinger, were putting the lives of POWs on the end of their list of priorities. She said she had realized something about the government a long time ago:

> That is, that in spite of the pats on the back, the sympathetic words and promises that they will not forget the prisoners is not true. The prisoners are in fact way down on the priority list. Mr. Nixon could bring them all home if he would set a date for a withdrawal of all American forces from South Vietnam. But he will not negotiate in Paris because he has never intended to withdraw all American forces. He hopes to placate the American public with constant references to his "winding down of the war."

On Friday, August 6, 1971, the *Bangor Daily News* welcomed the Nixon family to Maine:

> It is a pleasure to welcome President Nixon and family to Maine. We regret it's to be only for a brief weekend holiday.
>
> We know the President will enjoy himself and hope the sampling of Maine summers will encourage him to return for a longer stay sometime. In fact, we'd like to see him set up a summer White House here. Maine is a restful haven in a hectic world. We cannot think of a better place for a heavily burdened President to refresh his spirit and clear his mind.

An invitation was sent to Nixon to attend the Maine seafoods festival in Rockland on Saturday. A crowd of fifty thousand people was expected to attend that weekend event.

The president and his family received many invitations to events in Maine that weekend, which time would not allow Nixon to attend. Officials of the Winthrop bicentennial celebration invited Nixon to their party. The Sea and Shore Fisheries Commissioner Ronald W. Green, James Warren, chairman of the Maine Sardine Council, and Elmer Wheeler, Festival President, wired an invitation to Nixon for their weekend event, letting the president know that he could compete in the sardine-packing contest.

"It might be well to caution you, that should you decide to actively vie for the title, you will be facing ten of the fastest and most dedicated women of their professions. Failure in the contest would automatically entitle you to membership in King Neptune's Royal Order of Sardine Dropouts."

With such short notice of the president's arrival, Bangor International Airport manager Peter D'Errico had been working overtime with Secret Service to secure the airport for President Nixon's visit. About fifty teenagers from the Parks and Recreation departments in both Bangor and Brewer volunteered their services as ushers and guides during the Friday arrival. A large banner reading "Welcome to Bangor Mr. President!" was erected by the Greater Bangor Area Chamber of Commerce.

On Friday, the crowd started arriving at the airport about 11:00 a.m. The Army National Guard band played for the large crowd, estimated to be between four thousand and ten thousand people. The Chandlers, an Orono family group, sang and played accordion while telling jokes. Officials of Maine's Republican party assisted law enforcement with the parking of the cars.

The Nixon family was greeted by Governor Curtis as they emerged from the presidential airplane. Nixon and Curtis stood at the bottom of the plane ramp and talked briefly.

"I hope I've boosted your Maine tourism," the president said to the governor.

On the small speakers' platform with President Nixon was his wife Pat, his daughter Julie, Governor Curtis, and Democratic Congressman William D. Hathaway. Julie stood beside her mother and was described as appearing modestly self-conscious.

President Nixon praised Maine's representatives in Washington. He spoke of the ongoing war. Mrs. Nixon, watching her husband closely on the stage, was misty-eyed as she listened to the president talk about the men who were fighting in Vietnam.

Signs protesting the Vietnam War or the national economic situation were barred from the area of the airport by police. Still, a few managed to sneak through. Soon, a group stood inside the airport with signs. At one point, according to witnesses, police charged the group and snatched away several of the signs, including one carried by a ten-year-old.

One sign read "Muskie for President." Most protest placards could not be read from more than a few feet away from the audience, except for one sign with a black skull and the message "Napalm kills."

As the president continued to speak, a group of protestors broke out in an anti-war chant, which was hardly audible over the applause of the crowd. If the president heard the chant, he gave no indication of it.

"He heard it all right," said one veteran member of the national press corps to a local reporter. "If there was one dissident in a crowd of ten thousand, he'd hear it. But he'd never let on."

Midway through Nixon's talk a few protestors found signs that had been confiscated by police. In a few minutes the signs reappeared. Once again police moved in.

At the conclusion of President Nixon's remarks, the Nixon family moved along the rope barriers and shook hands for fifteen minutes. Mrs. Nixon signed autographs and spent several minutes with Bryan Pelkey, the Maine Muscular Dystrophy Poster Child. Mrs. Nixon was the chairwoman of the Muscular Dystrophy Association's national committee.

As the Nixons worked their way down the rope line, a girl stood in the back row with a placard that read "Keep Maine Clean, Send Nixon Home."

Eyeing the sign, through the crowd came Paulette Morin of Orrington. The two girls' eyes locked. Each started shouting their contradictory opinions on Vietnam. As the two girls argued, a group of protestors surrounded them. Morin would not back down from her support of American involvement in the Vietnam war. A protestor threatened Morin with arrest. With tears streaming down Morin's face, the girls continued to argue.

Paulette Morin was a 1966 graduate of Sumner Memorial High School in East Sullivan. She was taking a six-month general secretarial course at Beal College in Bangor. Morin had a stepbrother in the Army but not overseas. One of her cousins was a helicopter pilot in Vietnam.

On Saturday President Nixon read an account in the *Bangor Daily News* of Paulette's argument with the war protestor. Saturday evening, White House Aide Robert Faus located Ms. Morin at her father's home in Orrington. Faus told her that the president was disgusted with the behavior of the protestors but that he chose to ignore them, according to Morin.

President Nixon took the time over the weekend to praise Morin personally by phone. Morin said that the president told her that he and Mrs. Nixon thought she had done the right thing. The president offered to help find Morin a job in Washington when she finished school.

"It was very overwhelming," said Morin.

"All they do is stand around on street corners," said Ms. Morin of the protestors. They don't try and get a job. They complain about pollution—they're so dirty they stink. Can you imagine one of them as President of the United States?"

"Every time I go into downtown Bangor and one of those hippies shoves a copy of Paine in my face, I want to belt him," said Kenneth Drake, Ms. Morin's father.

Police had restricted dissident placard carriers from entering the airport, insisting it was private property. A Native-American spectator listened to the argument over whether the airport land was public or private.

"My people were here first, and it's all right with me," he said

The arrival of the Nixon family caused the biggest traffic jam Bangor had ever seen. The crowd that had greeted President Nixon left the airport at the same time that people were arriving at the Bangor State Fair. There was also a softball game at the airport to further complicate matters, and a downpour was drenching the city streets. To complicate the traffic jam, a small boy ran into the side of a car at the corner of Lincoln and Main streets. The child was not injured.

The Nixons boarded Army Helicopter Number One at 6:05 p.m., and in a few minutes were headed for Minot Island and the home of Nixon friend Jack Dreyfus, a wealthy New York stockbroker.

Ten or more New England Telephone and Telegraph Company utility trucks were on Islesboro Friday morning rigging telephone equipment for the president. Central Maine Power sent a fully equipped truck and crew to spend three days on Islesboro on a standby basis, in part to ensure the proper functioning of two diesel generators that had been brought to Minot Island for the visit.

The Dreyfus estate did lose a flower garden due to test landings by a helicopter.

People on Islesboro were excited by Nixon's visit.

"I'm a registered Democrat, but Nixon will get my vote," said Frederick A. Pendleton, who had lived his entire seventy-four years on Islesboro.

"It's beautiful, the people are beautiful, everything is very congenial. Nixon spends too much time overseas. It's good he gets down with the local people," said Amy Rose, who had spent three consecutive summers on the island working for a wealthy summer family.

Others on Islesboro were not so excited. Kim Christiana was an employee of the Island Pub.

"Because there is no access to the President, I cannot get excited. I can't understand this big turmoil. I know a lot of people who would like to say something to him."

The Nixons spent the weekend cruising on Penobscot Bay aboard the *Marsi*, a twenty-eight-foot yacht put at Nixon's disposal by his host.

"We've got the whole party going," said a voice over a radio as the Nixons headed onto Penobscot Bay aboard the small cruiser. The president was dressed in a wine-colored jacket, blue shirt, and dark trousers. He stepped aboard the cruiser with the aid of a Secret Service agent.

Nixon's Secret Service code name was Searchlight. Pat Nixon was Starlight. Julie and David Eisenhower were Sahara and Starbonnet respectively.

The Nixons went down a metal dock to a small orange cruiser commanded by David Rolerson, a staffer on the summer estate. The family was going on a cruise to look at the islands in that section of Penobscot Bay. They were on the water for fifty-two minutes, from 3:05 p.m. to 3:57 p.m. At one point Nixon's son-in-law David Eisenhower took the helm, wearing a bright red short-sleeved shirt.

The *J. T. Morse* out of Searsport, captained by Nathan Trump, helped bring the press out to Penobscot Bay for pictures. Private press boats were kept at a distance by two Secret Service speedboats and several Coast Guard vessels. On Saturday, one of the press boats did get close, and the president gave permission for the others to follow for a few photographs.

The Nixon's cruise coincided with the Dark Harbor Twenties, a race of seven twenty-foot sloops. Many boats filled the water to catch a glimpse of the Nixon family. They were all rigged with full sail to salute the president.

The president had ordered forty lobsters for Saturday's dinner. On Sunday, the Nixons dined on more lobster. Lobster was a favorite of the Nixons, despite one of them pinching Mrs. Nixon's finger in 1952 at a campaign event in Rockland. The Nixons also ate native Maine corn, string beans, clams, and salad.

President Nixon had the normal amount of paperwork to do and phone calls to make during his visit. A special and elaborate phone system had been set up for the president's visit, involving microwave relays at nearby Islesboro and Bangor, and a special security telephone switchboard in Rockland. A hundred-foot tower to enable communications via a wireless telephone system was erected.

On the island with Nixon were several of his aides, with whom he conferred several times. One of the items Nixon worked on in Maine was his welcoming remarks for the Apollo 15 astronauts. The president congratulated them by phone from Minot Island.

On Saturday night the Nixon family enjoyed a private viewing of the film *A Fistful of Dollars*.

Senator Smith arrived in Bangor around 5:30 p.m. on Sunday aboard a Navy transport from Brunswick Naval Air Station. About fifteen minutes later, the Nixons arrived from Minot Island aboard a helicopter, their weekend vacation complete. The first family was described as appearing tanned and generally relaxed.

"It was an island of enchantment," said Mrs. Nixon.

"We had lobster every meal," said President Nixon. "My daughter Julie dug for clams and we had them steamed. It's a great vacationland. I got lots of sun today. I've had vacations in Maine three times. That's pretty good for a Californian."

Senator Smith joined President Nixon for nearly half an hour of handshaking at the airport before the Nixon family departed. Nixon stopped to talk to airline flight attendants, telling them they were going to be very busy in the upcoming months during the political campaign. Before the Nixons left, Brewer Mayor Rudolph Marcous gave Mrs. Nixon a key to his city.

"I don't know if the president has a key to the City of Bangor," Marcoux said to Mrs. Nixon, "but here's one from the people of Brewer."

Mrs. Nixon smiled and said she would make sure the president got the key.

More than 1,500 people were at the airport to see the state's weekend guests off. *The Spirit of '76* left BIA at approximately 6:15 p.m., bound for Washington, DC. Senator Smith hitched a ride.

On Monday, July 1, 1974, a month before resigning from office, the White House announced that in two days, President Nixon would arrive at Loring Air Force Base in Limestone at 7:00 p.m. and deliver a major nationwide address on his visit to the Soviet Union, from where he was returning. The president was then to depart for Key Biscayne, Florida, for the Independence Day holiday. His speech from Loring was to be broadcast by the three television networks—ABC, CBS, and NBC, as well as radio.

Congressman William Cohen was the only Republican member of the Maine Congressional delegation. He was not invited to greet the president at the Loring arrival. Cohen could not have attended, even if he'd wanted to; he was in Washington considering articles of impeachment against the president. Cohen only found out about the visit when an administrative assistant called him Sunday night after hearing a Washington newscast.

"It's kind of surprising that he will deliver his major address from Loring," Cohen said. "But I don't believe it will put any pressure on me and my job with Judiciary. The only pressure I have is going over the evidence and determining what is meant by an impeachable offense. The consequences of what I will do is the only thing on my mind these days."

Not all Republicans were enthusiastic about Nixon's visit. Mrs. Marilyn King, president of the Women's Civic Club, said that her group had not planned anything because she had heard the visit was only open to base personnel. She said her group would have a presence at the arrival. There was not much excitement over the visit because the president had lost so much prestige in his own country, said King. The club did help spruce up the base for the visit.

"I don't care what you think of the guy—he's still President. I think he still has some strong supporters up here," said Bruce Billings, a Limestone attorney.

John Tiernan, chairman of the Aroostook County Republican Committee, released a statement urging "all of the people of the county, regardless of political persuasion, to come out to Loring" to welcome the president.

At Loring Air Force Base, the motto was "If it moves, salute it; if it doesn't, paint it." It was estimated that 2,400 hours had been put into the preparation, at a cost of $100,000. A six-year veteran of the Air Force was interviewed before the visit. He said the point was to impress not the president, who knew full well he was in an airport hangar, but to impress the media and the public who would attend.

Civilians were brought in to help out, including high school students. They were reportedly paid time and a half. Lawns were mowed, floors were waxed by hand, curbstones were band-brushed and painted, and litter was picked up from beside the roads. The base said it was simply concentrating its summer spruce-up efforts into a short time period.

Signs were placed throughout the base. On a flatbed trailer sat a sign that read "Welcome home Mr. President, from the people of the Loring community. Like you, peace is our profession." Civic groups and town officials in Limestone swung into action.

On the day of the presidential visit, base employee David Schwarz reported to work at 5:30 a.m., and when he got out of work, he went directly to the arrival site, where he stood waiting for over five hours. Schwarz did get to shake the hands of President Nixon and Vice President Ford.

The gates of Loring Air Force Base were opened to the public at 4:30 p.m. on Wednesday, July 3, 1974. The people of New Brunswick had also been invited to the president's arrival. Hundreds of people literally ran to get a front-line spot on the ropes. There were about five thousand in the crowd, standing room only. The areas closest to the podium were off limits to anyone who did not have a military pass.

Two bands played: the Fort Fairfield High School Stage Band and the Caribou High School Marching Band. The Fort Fairfield group had just learned on Friday that they would play and had been "practicing like crazy" since then.

President Nixon arrived at 7:30 p.m. People jostled for position to get a photograph.

President Nixon was greeted by Maine Governor Kenneth Curtis. Vice President Gerald Ford flew into Loring to introduce the president. Ford quoted the Bible in his introduction. "Blessed are the peacemakers," said Ford.

A banner behind the president read "Welcome Home, Mr. President." When Ford introduced Nixon, he accidentally called him "Mr. Speaker."

In the back of the hangar people continued to talk as Nixon spoke, causing a constant murmur that could be heard at all times. Nixon described his welcome as "splendid." "It is always good to come home to America," said Nixon.

> Governor Curtis and Mrs. Curtis, and to all our great friends here in Maine, I want to thank you for giving us such a pleasant welcome as we return. I know that, as I see cars parked, what a real effort it is to come out to an air base. It took a lot of time and we appreciate that effort and we thank you very much. And to each and every one of you and to perhaps millions who are listening on television and radio, I can assure you of one thing, and that is, it's very good to come home to America.

Nixon said that agreements achieved during his meeting with the Soviet Union would advance the cause of peace. "It is clear to the leaders of the Soviet Union we will not proceed at the expense of our traditional allies."

President Nixon talked for twenty minutes to the enthusiastic crowd that was jammed into a hanger near the Loring flight line, which was being broadcast live nationally.

Nixon announced three major agreements on arms systems between the Soviet Union and the United States. The president said a new agreement had been signed in the area of offensive strategic weapons, which he said brought closer a final accord on strategic arms. Nixon did not give specifics of any of the agreements. He also reflected on the upcoming Independence Day holiday: "As we prepare tomorrow to celebrate the anniversary of that independence—the 198th anniversary, we as Americans can be proud that we have been true to Jefferson's vision, and that as a result of America's initiative, that universal goal of peace is now closer—closer not only for ourselves, but for all mankind. Thank you very much and good evening."

At the end of the speech, Nixon stepped down from the podium and checked quickly with his Secret Service men. Upon getting a nod, Nixon began greeting the airmen and dependents in the front sections. He chatted with the members of the Fort Fairfield band and the Caribou band. The president spent about five minutes after his remarks shaking hands. It was said that Nixon seemed to relish the warm reception.

At the door of the hanger, Mrs. Nixon was presented with a bouquet of yellow roses by seven-year-old Joyce Emma Pavio, the daughter of one of the servicemen stationed at Loring. Mrs. Nixon thanked the girl with a kiss on the cheek.

During the speech, outside the hangar, thirty-five Native Americans from the Malecite Reservation in Perth, New Brunswick, danced in "peaceful demonstration." Children danced a dance showing their feelings, which, it was explained, were that they wanted Nixon to recognize and help the Native Americans.

The demonstrators carried placards, which were not allowed inside the hangar. "Nixon, you're on Our Land," "Plant that Tree on Indian Land," "Clear up Your Dirt for ME," "Send Henry to our Reserves," and "Reactors for the Arabs and a Fat Zero for the Indian." One child carried a banner that read "My father fought for you in Vietnam."

Because the placards were not allowed inside the hangar, the Native Americans decided to set the demonstration outside the structure.

"Everybody has a voice in America except the Indian," said Louis Sapiere, Sr.

Several hundred people left the hangar to watch the demonstration. The demonstrators stayed until the entire crowd had left the hangar after the president's speech. Three people danced in the center of a semi-circle comprised of Native Americans. "They are dancing of a free heart," said Sapiere. "This is what they feel; the Indian needs a voice in America."

Some people simply walked through the demonstration. One person said the Native American demonstrators would do "anything for publicity." Another person remarked to one of the Native American demonstrators, "You must be a newsman."

The *Bangor Daily News* summed up the day.

> For those in the crowd, some of whom had stood waiting for hours, others whom had spent days cutting grass and painting everything from curbstones to steam pipes, it was the kind of day that was worth it all. But it was the kind of day that many were relieved to see over, so that life at the northern Maine air force base at Limestone could get back to normal.

After the president's visit, the newspaper noted that many national reporters put Caribou as their dateline.

"But Limestone residents took the error in good stride, figuring that whether the President knew he was in Limestone or may later think he was in Caribou, he was in *the county.*"

After President Nixon resigned from the office just a month later, he defended his record, quoting from President Theodore Roosevelt's 1910 speech, "Citizenship in a Republic":

> Sometimes I have succeeded and sometimes I have failed, but always I have taken heart from what Theodore Roosevelt once said about the man in the arena, "whose face is marred by dust

and sweat and blood, who strives valiantly, who errs and comes up short again because there is not effort without error and short-coming, but who does actually strive to do the deed, who knows the great enthusiasms, the great devotions, who spends himself in a worthy cause, who at the best knows in the end the triumph of high achievements and who at the worst, if he fails, at least fails while daring greatly."

Gerald R. Ford

The circumstances of Gerald Ford's succession to the presidency of the United States would cast a shadow on his two-and-a-half years in office. He was sworn into office on August 9, 1974, after the resignation of President Richard Nixon.

President Ford would pardon President Nixon for his part in the Watergate scandal, which grew out of a botched break-in of the Democratic National Committee, and the attempt at a coverup of the crime. That decision would haunt him during his presidential election campaign, as would a bad economy, growing inflation, and a dispirited country.

President Ford's visit was on August 30, 1975. After breakfast at the White House on that Saturday morning, the president attended to business briefly in the Oval Office before heading to the South Grounds and entering an awaiting helicopter, which flew Ford to Andrews Air Force Base in Maryland. The president and his party would arrive at Brunswick Naval Air Station in at 9:00 a.m.

Greeting President Ford were base commander Captain Robert L. Latta, Maine Governor James B. Longley, an Independent, along with the governor's wife Helen and their five children. Also greeting the president were John Linnell, Chairman of the Maine Republican State Committee, and Hattie Bickmore, Vice Chairman of the Maine Republican State Committee.

President Ford, accompanied by Governor Longley and Longley's son James B. Longley, Jr., motored to Augusta, where the president participated in a field day program sponsored by the Maine American Federation of Labor and Congress of Industrial Organizations (AFL-CIO). The event, held at the Augusta Civic Center, was for the benefit of the Pineland Hospital and Training Center.

At the civic center, President Ford was greeted by Benjamin Dorsky, president of the Maine AFL-CIO; David Elvin, mayor of Augusta; Lionel Dubay, director of the Augusta Civic Center; and Paul Poulin, city manager of Augusta.

Dorsky would escort President Ford to the holding room arranged in the civic center, where he was greeted by Maine's congressional delegation, including Senator Edmund Muskie, (Democrat), Senator William Hathaway (Democrat), Congressman David Emery (Republican), and Congressman William Cohen (Republican), who had served on the House Judiciary Committee, whose investigation of charges against President Nixon had led to the president's resignation.

President Ford was also greeted by State Representative Neil Rolde (Democrat) and State Representative Barry Hobbins (Democrat).

The president was presented with a petition requesting that Maine manufacturers retain the government contract for the M-60 machine gun.

Dorsky then escorted President Ford to the offstage announcement area of the Civic Center before being introduced by Governor Longley.

President Ford addressed approximately 6,500 persons at the program. His remarks from Augusta were broadcast live by state television stations.

Dorsky then escorted the president to his awaiting motorcade. Accompanied by Congressmen Cohen and Emery, President Ford was driven to the Holiday Inn on Spring Street in Portland. He was greeted by Portland Mayor Harold Loring and various other officials. Mayor Loring would present President Ford with a key to the city of Portland and read a proclamation declaring August 30, 1975 as "President Ford Day in Portland."

The president would spend about a half an hour in a suite that had been arranged for him before being escorted to the Androscoggin room at 12:30 p.m., the guest of honor at a reception for approximately fifty Maine Republican contributors. President Ford would then meet privately with a few invited guests. Later he attended a Republican fundraising luncheon in the same hotel. After addressing approximately six hundred guests, President Ford was presented with a wood sculpture of an American oyster catcher, carved by artist Charles "Chippy" Chase of Brunswick.

President Ford was taken by motorcade to the Portland International Jetport, where he left for another event in Rhode Island.

James E. Carter

And I'm sure that you were treated well during your stay last night with the Bob Murray family on Maple Street, as fine an Irish Roman Catholic family as ever was imbued with the Protestant work ethic.

—*Bangor Daily News*

President James Earl Carter was born at the hospital in Georgia where his mother worked as a registered nurse. He served in the Navy, working in the nuclear submarine program. He went on to serve as the governor of Georgia. On his second day in office, Carter pardoned all Vietnam War draft evaders.

President Carter came to Maine on February 18, 1978, for a fundraising dinner and a town-hall meeting. It was a difficult time for Maine, which was dealing with the issue of the Indians Land Claim lawsuit.

The Indian Land Claim lawsuit involved a federal lawsuit on behalf of several Native-American tribes in the state of Maine, who said their federal rights had been violated over the years and that they had a claim on two thirds of the state's private property.

President Carter arrived at the Bangor International Airport at 6:20 p.m. He was greeted by Governor James B. Longley and members of the state's congressional delegation.

Just five minutes before the presidential jet touched down in Bangor, a two-car crash on Union Street tied up traffic for a good distance. Three people were treated and later released from Eastern Maine Medical Center.

The president was dressed in a white trench coat and no hat. He was described as appearing well rested. A light snow greeted President Carter and fell on him as he went through the official reception line at the airport. The press was allowed on the runway, but no spectators were allowed on the closely secured international arrivals runway abutting the Air National Guard base.

First in the reception line was Governor and Mrs. James B. Longley, followed by Bangor Mayor Arthur Brountas.

"Hello, Mr. Mayor," Carter said to Brountas.

Congressman William Cohen was next in the reception line. Cohen had not been invited aboard Air Force One on the trip to Maine and so had to take a privately chartered plane. At the airport, state treasurer Leighton Cooney got in trouble with the Secret Service, but Cohen came to his rescue.

Just before the president's airplane arrived, Cooney's white Volkswagen breached a security line. Two Secret Service men pounced on the vehicle and held Cooney. Cohen spotted him and told the agents he could identify his former political adversary.

A twenty-car entourage, including the president, dignitaries, television cameras documenting the event, and city and state police sped from the runway, along with a city of Bangor ambulance, through gates 1 and 2, where the motorcade was greeted by about a hundred or so spectators.

The president went directly to the Penobscot Valley Country Club to attend a fund-raising cocktail party. An honor guard of students from Maine Maritime Academy in Castine stood outside the new door of the club, waiting for the president. Inside, $7,000 worth of new carpeting had been laid for the visit by brothers Albert and Bud Gallant.

The event was a $500-a-plate dinner. At about 5:50 p.m. the diners were summoned to dinner in the dining room. There was a staff of ten servers and the cooking crew. The guests ate roast tenderloin of beef.

At 7:10 p.m. President Carter descended to the dining room from a holding room upstairs. He was greeted in the receiving line by nineteen-year-old Martha Muskie, daughter of Senator Edmund Muskie. She presented the president with a letter from a dozen three- and four-year-old children enrolled in the nursery school program at the University of Maine at Orono, where Ms. Muskie was a sophomore.

The letter read: "Dear Mr. President: We love you. Thank you for coming to Orono. Say hello to Amy."

The president was also given a copy of *Bangor, Maine—An Illustrated History,* and he received a gift for his daughter, Amy—a copy of *Down East to Bangor* by Julia Eaton.

Carter spoke to the crowd for more than fifteen minutes, with most of his remarks aimed at praising Maine's Senator William Hathaway, describing him as "a man for all seasons who has gained the admiration and respect of all Americans and leaders abroad."

Not everyone was at the function to support Hathaway; many were Republicans, and many just wanted to meet the president.

Some people balked at the expensive fundraiser, including Mrs. Herbert Dowling of Whitneyville in a letter to the editor of the *Bangor Daily News*:

> I realize that his visit to Bangor is a fund-raising project in behalf of Sen. William Hathaway, but for $500 a plate who can afford to attend? Certainly not the farmers like my husband and I from Washington County! I am wondering if that isn't on the borderline of discriminating against the average citizen, for as I see it, only the elite can afford to attend. Once again the average middle class, hard-working person is the one who is paying the bills for this country and left standing on the outside looking in.

The *Bangor Daily News* featured a cartoon with Carter's famous smile over the Bangor Standpipe.

"He brings with him three pretty good size Maine-inspired headaches, all emanating from the same geographical area of our beloved state: The Indian land claims thing, which, one must admit, is a bit of a doozy; the proposed Dickey-Lincoln hydroelectric project, another pretty good bellringer; and the future of Limestone's Loring Air Force Base, a situation that has the natives growing restless," wrote the *Bangor Daily News*.

There were over three thousand people at the Bangor Auditorium awaiting President Carter's arrival from Orono. After the fundraising dinner, the president and his motorcade made their way to the auditorium for the town hall meeting. The marquee outside the auditorium gave England Dan and John Fogerty, who would be appearing in concert there in a few days, top billing over the president. The words "Welcome President Carter" were under those of the popular musical duo.

An editorial cartoon in the *Bangor Daily News* on the 17th showed a picture of a man with Native American feathered headdress with a piece of paper that read "Provide Indian Claim Settlement to Please Everyone." The caption read "How."

A Frightened Maine

Welcome to Bangor, Mr. President,

We are honored by your visit. It is not often that Mainers in this neck of the woods get to see and even talk first hand with the President of the United States. We hope you enjoy your overnight stay with the Murray family, and see enough of our magnificent state to lure you back again some time.

Listen to us while you're here, too. Please.

Maine is a deeply troubled and confused state right now. The chief source of our discomfort is, of course, the Indian land claims suit—the Penobscot and Passamaquoddy Indians' claim to 12 million acres of Maine wildlands.

For most of us, the Indian land suit has persisted as a grave dilemma that is, by its magnitude and complexity, both fearful and frustrating. Because most decent hardworking Maine people consider it incredible that this Indian thing could unfold the way it has, and because of a popular distrust and suspicion that we are being misused by Washington politics, and because we cannot come to feel morally beholden or legally responsible for granting economic independence to our tribes, our adrenalin has been working overtime since your White House staff announced its "solution" to this strange legal albatross.

Some of what you propose is intimidating enough to be both frightening and appalling. And, as you are learning with your Middle east worries, both fear and intimidation evoke negative human responses; We in Maine don't like being put up against the wall by the great White Father any better than the Wabanaki nation did.

By unilaterally suggesting, as one part of your Indian land claims settlement, that 14 of Maine's largest landowners surrender 300,000 acres of timberland to the two tribes, your staff is toying with a form of governmental expropriation, or the next thing to it. We in this state view that specific recommendation as a coercive attempt to invade the sanctity of property ownership.

And to exclude all landowners below 50,000 acres does little to ameliorate the violation. . . . If it is wrong for Maine's small landowner to surrender property at the government behest, it is just as wrong to ask big landowners to ante up acreage.

We are a modest sort up here, and not always wise to the ways of power politics and constitutional law, neither are we unprincipled suckers (catfish down your way) willing to bite the first expedient bait that is introduced.

Outside the Bangor Auditorium, a group of Maine women hoped to present the president with a list of four top-priority items that they felt were important issues to the women of the state.

The group was comprised of members of various women's organizations and members of the Maine delegation to the National Women's Conference. One of the women was Cynthia Murray Beliveau, daughter of *the* Robert Murray, at whose house the president was staying for the night.

The group's list encouraged the president to work for the passage of the Equal Rights Amendment. They hoped the president would include the topic of the ERA in one of his fireside chats. They also wished to encourage him to continue to accelerate appointments of women to judiciary and top-level policy-making positions. They wanted assistance for displaced homemakers in the form of re-education opportunities and funding for shelter for battered women and children.

"We're going to have some wine and warm up," said one of the ERA demonstrators outside the Bangor Auditorium Friday night.

A planned demonstration regarding the Indian Land Claim settlement proposal never materialized.

The number of Secret Service and White House employees at the auditorium topped three hundred. They stayed in 150 motel rooms, using forty or fifty rental cars, eating at dozens of local restaurants in the Bangor area. The bill was expected to reach $50,000.

Approximately fifty people were used as volunteers to help set up for the visit. Duties included drawing names of people to be audience members, taking calls, handling tickets.

As citizens entered the auditorium, they were greeted by the tunes of the Bangor High School Band. Some of their offerings had a pronounced Native-American beat. A cardboard sign read "All Bags And Purses Must Be Searched Here." It was propped on a table where the bags and purses could be laid for search.

Local television and radio stations prepared and fine-tuned their equipment to cover the remarks of the president. The press was kept in a specific bull pen and was not allowed to mingle with the crowd.

Attendees at the town hall meeting were drawn by lottery. Mariette Collins of Aroostook County had her name picked but was not allowed to have the tickets. She had filled out an application for tickets, her application had been drawn on Tuesday, and her name had been published in the final editions of the *Bangor Daily News* Wednesday. Mrs. Collins was working at the K-Mart in Madawaska when a friend told her she had seen her name in the paper.

"I'm going to find out why even if I have to write to Washington to do it," said Collins.

It turned out that President Carter's town hall was for Penobscot County residents only. Mrs. Collins said she was "terribly hurt" that she did not get to see President Carter.

"They shouldn't have published my name if they didn't want me," Mrs. Collins told Beurmond Banville, St. John Valley Bureau reporter for the *Bangor Daily News.*

Mrs. Collins was further disappointed when she requested the ticket as a souvenir. She was told on the phone that the ticket would be given to someone else and she could not have it.

"It really bothered me to be refused."

In the end, the coordinator for the ticketing process mailed Mrs. Collins two unused tickets.

Others objected to the lottery system. David Daniels of Orono wrote a letter to the editor of the *Bangor Daily News* in protest.

"Lottery my foot! I bet the first 2,000 of those Carter town hall tickets go to councilmen, commissioners, ward heelers, card pushers, hangers on, gophers, and every other political hack in Penobscot County and surroundings. My bet is you could submit an attendance list today and be ninety percent correct!"

Carter entered the Bangor Auditorium at exactly 8:00 p.m., welcomed by loud cheers and sustained applause. He was cheered again during his opening remarks when he said his brother Billy might come to Maine someday.

President Carter walked up to the podium specially designed for him and mounted an oval dais. He was dressed in a dark blue suit with a light blue shirt and patterned maroon necktie. An American flag was in the buttonhole of his left lapel. On the podium, to his right was an American flag, to his left was the State of Maine flag. People stood on chairs to see Carter.

"This reminds me of 1976, in the latter part of the campaign, not the first part, when I came to Maine for the first time. No one knew who I was, or cared. I made a speech to the Democratic State Convention—and I remember that I was the twenty-third person on the program. I started speaking about 10:20," said President Carter.

"Then when I began to run for president, and came back, some of you were very hospitable to me and took me in and made me feel at home. Later my wife came, but three sons, their wives, my aunt Cissy, my sister Ruth, my mother, and maybe later maybe Billy would come as well."

"It was a friendly, almost personal crowd, and almost all of them greeted him warmly," said the *Bangor Daily News* reporter Arthur B. Layton, Jr.

Carter said he got involved in the Indian Land Claims lawsuit "very reluctantly," and only did so because the lawsuit had the potential to tie up every piece of Maine land, with none of it being able to be bought or sold for years.

"I could foresee some very serious consequences happening in Maine," said Carter.

He said that he could have done nothing and "let the people of Maine sweat it out."

"You don't have to take the deal if you don't want it," President Carter told the crowd. "I felt that so many people were affected by the suit in Maine . . . that it was a special case. But I hope this is the only such case I become involved in."

Carter made it clear during the town hall that he would not sign any legislation that would totally extinguish aboriginal Native-American claims as an overall solution to the Indian Land Claims suit.

During the question-and-answer portion of the evening, Bill Hussey of Bath thanked the president for the contracts that enabled Bath Iron Works to operate.

Wayne Bayer of Bangor asked about affordable health care.

James Clark asked about mental health care.

Ed Meadows of Hamden asked about the steps the Carter Administration would take to ensure wood energy would play a prominent role in federal energy policy.

Bobby Burr from Old Town asked how the Democratic Party could call themselves the champions of the poor, oppressed and elderly while drastically cutting aid for those groups and giving themselves a raise.

Paul Perdikis of Bangor asked the president what he was going to do about the situation in Cyprus.

Joan Holmberg of Maple Street in Bangor asked about malpractice reform.

Mary Smith of Bangor asked if the president felt he had put more women in decision-making positions than "your unenlightened Republican predecessors."

Jerry Thibodeau of Bangor asked about abortion.

Chris Cookson of Brewer asked where the president planned to get oil if the Middle East refused to sell to the United States.

A teacher from Hampden asked about the president's plan to implement a separate department of education.

One question that was asked, which received loud and long applause, was this:

"Since our land claims case will set a precedent across the country, will other states have to be as lucrative in the giving of land and money as we are in the state of Maine?"

As part of down-home style of the Carter presidency, it was announced that during his stay in Maine, President Carter would forgo a hotel stay to be a guest in a private Bangor residence.

Jo-Marie Prescott, eleven, of Hampden, wrote to the *Bangor Daily News,* offering Carter a place to stay during his visit.

"I read in your newspaper on Feb. 6 that people don't have room for President Jimmy Carter to stay with them. Will you invite him to come to my house? We will make room for him. He can sleep in my nice canopy bed, and we heat our house with wood. I would let him help me fill the wood box."

The president ended up staying at the home of Robert Murray, the father-in-law of Severin Beliveau, counsel for the Save Loring Committee.

There were disruptions in the neighborhood where President Carter stayed. Arthur Nagelini, who lived on Mt. Hope Avenue, was able to get through a Secret Service blockade to report to work at 5:30 p.m., but had to leave at his 10:00 p.m. lunch hour because the Secret Service told him they would prefer he not drive into the neighborhood after his normal workday, which ended at 2:00 a.m.

Nagelini had planned to go ice fishing the day after the president's visit, and he planned to leave at 7:00 a.m. The Secret Service told him he would have to leave either before 6:30 a.m. or after 8:00 a.m. in order to not disrupt the presidential departure plans from the neighborhood.

Donald Taylor, who lived directly next to the Murrays, decided to skip work altogether. He said he was allowed to come and go as he pleased but had decided to stay home. Taylor said there were Secret Service men all around and added that he could not say if that meant they were in his house as well as outside.

Busloads of local school children had been stopping by the house throughout the day, their teachers using the visit as an impromptu educational lesson. Taylor said everyone in town had been up and down Maple Street during the visit.

"It has been like downtown New York City," Taylor told a *Bangor Daily News* reporter.

The Taylors made known their support for Republican William Cohen by spreading a white bed sheet across the front of their home on Maple Street, next to an American flag. "Welcome to Cohen Country" read the sheet.

More than three hundred people turned out in the Maple Street neighborhood when President Carter arrived at the Murray home that evening. He was welcomed by loud cheers and applause.

Carter quickly broke from the Secret Service line and greeted people individually. He kissed and hugged a few infants and shook hands with whoever could stick a hand in his direction. The majority of the crowd were school children, who clapped their mittened hands together as Carter came toward them.

Ann Ellis of Veazie was visiting friends directly across the street from the Murrays.

"No matter what party you're affiliated with, seeing a president this close is something special. . . . [I]t kind of reminds you of what we have here in this country."

Traffic was blocked off for two blocks down Maple Street and one block in either direction along Mount Hope Avenue. Carter walked onto the steps of the Murray home, and Mr. Murray and his wife came onto the well-lit porch to greet their visitor. Mrs. Murray expected a handshake, extending her hand. However, Carter embraced and kissed her. Then the president turned to face the crowd on Maple Street, waved goodnight, wiped his feet on a black porch mat, and entered the house. Spectators milled about for a bit and then went home to watch themselves on the news.

"He's the most natural person in the world," Mrs. Murray told the News. "He wasn't in the house two minutes and he became a member of the family."

Carter did have a helping of Mrs. Murray's famous date nut pudding, which earned his seal of approval. Murray's son-in-law Severin Beliveau said the pudding should be put on the White House menu.

"Maine's Four Seasons" was a booklet that was prepared by the Mary Snow School's second grade. The booklet was presented by teacher Jeanne Campo to Robert Murray, the president's host. The cover page of the large booklet read "For President Carter because we like you!" Storer Boone, who was a thirteen-year-old living on Maple Street, gave Mrs. Murray a Bangor Youth Hockey bumper sticker to give to the president.

The president went upstairs to bed between 11:15 and 11:30 p.m., about ninety minutes after arriving at the Murray home. The room in which Carter stayed was described as having a Lincolnesque atmosphere, with a chunky dark-stained desk, bureau, matching wood-framed mirror, and small night table, and olive and gold small masculine printed wallpaper. A bright gold short shag rug was on the floor, a plain gold cotton bedspread covering the double bed.

"It's okay for the president to use the desk," said Frank Murray, the hosts' son who normally occupied the room. "In fact, if he wants to carve his initials in it, too, that's even better.

The house had only one bathroom. The president's wife and his personal physician were staying at the home of Beth Largay, about six houses down from the Murrays. President Carter checked in with his wife, Rosalyn, by telephone before going to sleep. Downstairs, Mr. and Mrs. Murray tiptoed around, putting the house back in order after the president's retirement for the evening.

"We're ecstatic . . . it's a feeling we're not able to put into words," said Laura Murray.

At about 4:00 a.m. security officials were given a jolt when a drunk driver drove down Maple Street from Stillwater Avenue, smashing through a blockade at Maple and Mount Hope Avenue. He skidded past the closely guarded house. The motorist, who was traveling alone, was interrogated and taken to jail. It was unknown whether the incident woke up the president.

President Carter received his official wake-up call from the White House switchboard at 6:30 a.m. From 7:46 to 7:54 the president talked

with Secretary of Labor F. Ray Marshall. Spectators had already gathered behind the barricades outside the Murray home. The Murrays had
gotten up at 5:45 and prepared breakfast for eleven diners.

"I wanted to make bacon and eggs and the whole thing for him,"
said Mrs. Murray. "He eats light—all the time."

The breakfast table was decorated with unlit white candles and the
family's best silver. There was a fruit platter, orange juice, coffee, blueberry muffins made by Karen Richards of Winthrop, English muffins,
cheese, and a crumb coffee cake made by Mary Lou Arms of Brewer.

Mr. Murray offered grace before the meal, which was the fam-
ily's tradition. The group included Mr. and Mrs. Murray; President
Carter; his appointment secretary, Tim Kraft, who'd slept in an adjoin-
ing bedroom; Cynthia Ann Murray-Beliveau and her husband Severin
of Wayne; Buddy, a Murray son who was a Boston College freshman;
Frank, a Catholic University seminarian in Washington; Kathleen
Murray, a registered nurse in Fort Lauderdale, Florida; and Winifred
Murray-Higgins and her husband of Brewer. The president and the
Murrays talked mostly of their families over breakfast. Because son
Frank was returning to Washington on Saturday, Carter insisted he
catch a ride on Air Force One.

Carter greeted the crowd when he stepped out on the porch.

"You all get up pretty early around here," Carter said.

Many neighbors agreed that it was an honor to have a president
staying in their neighborhood. Though the crowd was smaller than the
day before, it was enthusiastic.

"It sounded like a football game out there," said Mrs. Beliveau.

After President Carter left, Maple Street returned to normal.

Maple Street resident Ray Bradford said the visit caused minimal
disturbance for everyone concerned.

"It's the most exciting thing that's happened on Maple Street in at
least a week," said Bradford.

For hours after the president left, cars continued to travel up and
down Maple Street, catching a glimpse of where the president of the
United States had slept.

Before leaving Maine, President Carter attended a fundraising
breakfast at Husson College. The president met with labor officials and

students at the Dickerman Dining Commons. The breakfast was a fundraiser for Senator Hathaway.

The visit delayed the opening of the Eastern Maine High School basketball tournament, being held at Husson.

Kent Ward, in his column Maine Politics in the Saturday edition of the *Bangor Daily News*, gave President Carter a morning greeting, "Morning, Mr. President . . . and I'm sure that you were treated well during your stay last night with the Bob Murray family on Maple Street, as fine an Irish Roman Catholic family as ever was imbued with the Protestant work ethic."

When they returned to their Maple Street home after seeing the president off at the airport, Laura Murray picked up the linen napkin the president had used and gave it a gentle hug.

"It's all hitting me now," she said.

On a white linen-covered oak table in the Murray's home, President Carter had left his hosts a special gift, an ornate blue and gold scrapbook. It was to hold the newspaper clippings of the president's visit. The president left the following note on one of the first pages.

"To Bob and Laura and all the Murrays, thank you for the new friendships and wonderful hospitality to me, the dozens of photographs and the hundreds of visitors. You all will have to come and see me and my family at the White House. Love, Jimmy Carter."

16

George H.W. Bush and George W. Bush

It's where my family comes home, it's our anchor to windward.

—President George H. W. Bush

George Herbert Walker Bush was the forty-first president of the United States. Bush married Barbara Pierce, and together the couple had six children. One of their sons, George Walker Bush, would also be elected president.

The Bush compound on Walker's Point in Kennebunkport, Maine, has been owned by the Bush family since the 1870s, when it was purchased by the senior President Bush's great-great-grandfather. George H. W. Bush had owned it since the 1970s.

The compound consists of the Bush summer home and eight other buildings, with homes for all of George H. W. Bush's children and their families. The compound, which is located on a spit of rocky land that juts out into the Atlantic Ocean, contains a swimming pool, tennis court, art studio, and horseshoe pit. The elder President Bush spent part of every summer at Walker's Point since his childhood, with the exception of his time as a pilot in the United States Navy during World War II.

The Bush compound at Walker's Point was called the summer White House. The place, and the family, made Kennebunkport a household name. During his time in office, President George H. W. Bush entertained world leaders at Walker's Point, including Margaret Thatcher and Mikhail Gorbachev. The national colors would be hoisted in front of the compound when the president was there. In 2007 the younger President Bush used the compound to host the "lobster sum-mit" with Russian President Vladimir Putin. Both presidents Bush took Putin sailing and fishing.

"Fishing is good for the soul," said President George H. W. Bush. "Fishing is good for one person to get to know another."

In the years after the first Bush's presidency, George and Barbara would spend more and more time at Walker's Point, at times from May until October. In 2009 a group of Mr. Bush's friends placed a naval anchor at a spot overlooking Walker's Point in a tribute to the former president.

"Walker's Point is a home away from home, an anchor to wind-ward," President George H.W. Bush told the *Bangor Daily News* in 1990. "I cherish the time Barbara and I spend there."

In 1994, the senior President Bush was inducted into the Maine Baseball Hall of Fame. In his youth, Bush had played for Kennebunk Collegians, a group of college and prep school students who played similar teams around the state.

Mabel's Lobster Claw was a favorite Kennebunkport spot of George and Barbara. Mabel's is a non-descript seafood shack in Kennebunk-port. One wall is covered with photos of "41," as Bush was known. The president's favorite meal was lobster and homemade peppermint ice cream.

Just weeks after Barbara died, on April 17, 2018, residents of Ken-nebunkport lined the streets when President George H. W. Bush came for the last time to his summer home. He would die eight months later.

Bush died Friday evening, November 30, 2018. The next day resi-dents paid their respects by turning a scenic Atlantic Ocean overlook near Walker's Point into an impromptu memorial featuring Christmas wreaths, flags, and flowers. A steady stream of people visited the site. At Walker's Point the U.S. flag was half-staff.

President Bush's death occurred during a time called Christmas Prelude in Kennebunkport, so the area already had more visitors than usual. The Kennebunkport Historical Society Bush Gallery was packed with visitors all that day. They circulated a memorial book that was eventually given to the Bush Family.

The historical society had mementos including golf clubs, and the jumpsuit the president wore when he skydived on his ninetieth birthday, landing on the grounds of St. Ann's Episcopal Church in Kennebunkport.

On September 4, 1976, while driving near his family's summer home in Kennebunkport, George W. Bush was pulled over and was cited for driving under the influence of alcohol and was fined. His Maine driver's license was suspended for a time.

When the long-ago incident was made public, it nearly cost George W. Bush the presidential election. Bush said the event had a stabilizing effect on his life, forcing him to confront his use of intoxicating substances.

After the death of President George H. W. Bush, his chief of staff, Freddy Ford, issued a statement regarding the future of Walker's Point.

"Forty-one's wishes were for the family to enjoy his beloved Walker's Point for generations, and that's just what they'll do."

Barack Obama

I went with coconut.

—President Barack Obama

President Barack Hussein Obama was born in Honolulu, Hawaii, on August 4, 1961. He married Michelle Robinson, and together the couple had two daughters, Malia and Natasha, called Sasha.

President Obama began his political career as a community organizer in Chicago. While serving as a senator from the state of Illinois, Obama was elected as the nation's forty-fourth president in 2008.

The first two presidents of the United States to visit Maine were slaveholders. Barack Obama came to Maine as the first African American to hold that office.

Barack Obama's first visit to Maine as president of the United States was on Thursday, April 1, 2010, when he spoke in Portland in opposition of the proposed Republican repeal of his newly passed health care program, the so-called "Obamacare."

"It's been a week, folks," President Obama said to the crowd. "So, before we find out if people like health care reform, we should wait to see what happens when we actually put it into place."

Even before the president arrived, the Republican National Committee sent an email to the media proclaiming the president an "Anti-job Maine-iac."

"If they want to have that fight, I welcome that fight, because I don't believe the American people are going to put the insurance industry back in the driver's seat," President Obama told a cheering crowd in Maine's largest city.

Maine's two senators, Olympia Snowe and Susan Collins, both Republicans, were invited to the speech, but did not attend. Senator Collins was on a trip to Qatar and Europe on official business, and Senator Snowe had other commitments scheduled.

Senator Collins said that she hoped the president would use the visit to talk more about his plans to help create much-needed jobs and address the struggling economy. Snowe paid respect to the office that President Barack Obama represented. "It's always an honor and privilege to have the president of the United States visit our great state," said Senator Snowe in a press release.

On his next visit to Maine, the president brought along the entire Obama family. The visit of the Obama family to Mount Desert Island was announced by Congresswoman Chellie Pingree, who said it was a personal vacation, with no official appearances scheduled.

"I'm so glad they're coming to enjoy the beauty of the island so we can share our little neck of the woods," said Debbie Dyer, curator of the Bar Harbor Historical Society.

The weather on Mount Desert Island was sunny on Friday, July 16, 2010. The temperatures were in the 70s and 80s. The island had been abuzz since the news of President Obama's visit had been announced just a few days before.

On Friday morning President Obama and his family emerged from Air Force One at the Hancock County–Bar Harbor Airport with big smiles. Obama saluted and walked down the steps.

President Obama was greeted by Maine Governor John Baldacci and his wife Karen, Congressman Mike Michaud, and Bar Harbor Town Council Member Ruth Eveland. Baldacci told Obama the best places to get lobster and invited him to play golf.

"He said that he was really looking forward to this," said Governor Baldacci. "His visit is an opportunity to showcase Maine to the nation and the world; it's very exciting. I told him it was a great shot in the arm for us, and he said he intends to have a great time."

The Obamas were presented with several bags of Maine-made gifts, including baskets made by Passamaquoddy tribal weavers, stuffed Maine toys, L. L. Bean bags, University of Maine hockey caps, popcorn from

East Corinth, a balsam pillow, bottles of Poland Spring water, organic maple syrup, blueberry jam, Raye's mustard and pretzels, Gladstone's trail mix, Little Lad's herbal popcorn, chocolate-covered blueberries and cranberries, a *Dishing Up Maine* cookbook, as well as other books and postcards, and even a couple of cans of Moxie. The handmade baskets were from Governor William Nicholas of the Passamaquoddy Tribe. Many of the gifts were given in L. L. Bean tote bags.

The Obama daughters, Malia and Sasha, also received tote bags, called sea bags, which included books about Maine, stuffed animals representing Maine animals, water bottles, trail mix, and balsam pillows. Governor Baldacci told the Obamas the gifts represented a taste of Maine offerings.

Congressman Michaud briefly talked politics with the president, discussing Maine unemployment and problems with the railroad in northern Penobscot and Aroostook Counties.

The Obama family visited Acadia National Park and biked its historic carriage roads within an hour of landing in Maine. Over the weekend they visited the summit of Cadillac Mountain, toured the Bass Harbor Head Lighthouse and hiked to Ship Harbor. Their dog, Bo, was always with them.

President Obama often stopped to talk with local residents and tourists. At one point, in the center of Bar Harbor, the Obamas treated themselves to ice cream at the Mt. Desert Island Ice Cream shop.

"I went with coconut," said Obama. "This stuff is terrific. I strongly recommend it."

The Obamas had lobster for dinner at Stewman's in downtown Bar Harbor. The family took a short cruise of Frenchman Bay aboard a National Park Service boat, surrounded by five smaller, faster Coast Guard boats and other crafts. The president waved to the crowd.

At every stop, Obama patiently greeted the crowds, allowing people to have their picture taken with him.

"There are still famous and wealthy people all over the island, and their privacy is very much respected," said Craig Neff, owner of The Naturalist's Notebook, a shop in Seal Harbor, summer home of internationally famous Martha Stewart, among others. "If I were a billionaire, I would certainly appreciate it. It's always been that way."

On Saturday morning the Obamas visited the Bar Harbor Club on West Street and then took a walk to Bar Island, accessible by a strip of sand at low tide only. Lunch was dockside at the Claremont in Southwest Harbor, the tour of Bass Harbor Head Lighthouse and the hike on the Ship Harbor Nature Trail.

On the dock at the Claremont, Obama greeted hospice volunteer Abbey Danke, who was manning a table at the races. Obama approached her, noted her nametag, and said "Nice to see you, Abbey," giving her a hug.

"No, I did not get any pictures or autographs," said Danke. "Just did not think it was appropriate, since they were on vacation. A part of me thought to say, 'I know who you are. You don't know who I am. Would you like my autograph?' But I bit my tongue."

As the Obamas headed back to the awaiting cars of the motorcade, the people on the lawn of the Claremont gave them a round of applause.

The Obamas were greeted by cheering crowds wherever they went that weekend, despite the blockages the visit caused on the heavily congested island. All the roads on the island were full of people hoping to catch a glimpse of the president.

The president and Mrs. Obama had supper at the Bar Harbor restaurant Havana Saturday without the girls. The Obamas were at the restaurant for ninety minutes before slipping into an awaiting SUV shortly before 9:30 p.m., taking a side street back toward the hotel.

On Sunday, the Obamas left the Hancock County-Bar Harbor Airport just before 10:30 a.m. aboard an awaiting jet.

"The first family enjoyed their visit to Maine and they're thankful for the warm welcome they received from Mainers throughout the weekend," said Moira Mack, a White House spokeswoman in a statement issued Sunday night.

Bar Harbor and Mount Desert police, Hancock County Sheriff's deputies, Maine State Police troopers and Acadia National Park rangers and Secret Service all assisted in the security detail during the visit. Short of just one day, President Obama's visit to Mount Desert Island was exactly one hundred years after the visit to that spot by President Taft.

I was fortunate enough to be working as a reporter in Bar Harbor at the time of President Obama's visit. The place truly was buzzing with excitement with the upcoming visit.

Friday morning was beautiful. I was stationed at the visitor's center on Thompson's Island, just outside of Trenton. Knowing what the crush of traffic would be like and being uncertain of the security measures that might be in place, I arrived at the visitor's center early and waited.

There were already a few people there, but before long the place was packed. Traffic continued to flow along Route 3 and people found vantage points to see the president.

There was one interesting incident at the visitor's center. There were many people milling about, knowing the presidential motorcade would have to pass by to get on the island. There were two women, slightly less than middle aged, walking around together; they appeared to be tourists with fanny packs.

Shortly before the motorcade went through, traffic stopped. During this time one of the people waiting at the visitor's center decided to leave, hopping on a motorcycle, and roaring down the road toward the island. Immediately the two female tourists approached a park ranger, quietly giving the ranger an order that no further vehicles were to leave the visitor's center.

The plain, ordinary tourists were in fact plain-clothes Secret Service agents.

Shortly thereafter, the motorcade began to approach. A Maine State Police car was in the lead. Lights were flashing. Over the state police car's loudspeaker came the warning to stay away from the road. And then, in what seemed like a flash, the motorcade—a seemingly long motorcade—went through rapidly. One could not be sure which car contained President Obama and his family.

The excitement on the island only grew with the arrival of the Obama family. The crowd in Bar Harbor was enormous. People milled about, hoping to catch a glimpse of the president. Soon word was spreading on the first family's movements. They were in the park, they were hiking. No one knew where the Obamas would be at any given time, but once they showed up some place, the crowd would multiply exponentially.

At the offices of the *Bar Harbor Times*, the reporters were also try-ing to figure the president's movement, hoping to get a story and a picture. I and Amy DeMerchant, one of the advertising representatives, walked down to the wharf to do some scouting. There were people just milling about.

Looking at the people on the wharf, however, gave a clue. There was a group of four men. They were kind of dressed like tourists, but not quite. They were all dressed pretty much alike, not very fancy, but just a bit more semi-formal than the typical Bar Harbor tourist.

Hoping this was an advance team for an upcoming presidential stop, I was not disappointed. Almost out of nowhere came part of the motorcade that had delivered the president to the island. The cars moved quickly down West Street to the wharf. The herd of national reporters covering the visit suddenly appeared.

President Obama, his wife, and two daughters came zipping across Frenchman Bay, enjoying the sights by boat, being given a private sight-seeing tour by the superintendent of Acadia National Park, Sheridan Steele.

Watching the crowd seemed to be as interesting as watching the president.

There were other sights that weekend. One was outside of a Bar Harbor restaurant waiting for the Obamas to emerge after a meal. The presidential limousine and other vehicles waited outside of the restau-rant on West Street, and the crowd of onlookers was kept on the other side of the street. The memorable sight was seeing two of the Secret Ser-vice agents inspecting their machine guns by the limousine while they waited for the president. It seemed almost as if they wanted the crowd to see the weaponry, just as a reminder.

When the Obamas left on Sunday, it was not so much a let-down as it was a build-up, knowing that another chapter had been added to the rich history of Bar Harbor, Mount Desert Island, and the state of Maine.

President Barack Obama returned to Maine on Friday, March 30, 2012, during a campaign stop in South Portland. He spoke at the Southern Maine Community College. The speech was a fundraiser, with tickets available for $44 for students and $100 for members of the public. Afterward, President Obama was the guest of honor at a private fund-raising event at the Portland Museum of Art. Tickets for that event were a little more pricy. Guests of the function could meet the president and have their picture taken with him for $10,000.

Donald J. Trump

A week before the manuscript for this book was finally complete, news was announced that President Donald J. Trump would be visiting Maine.

As was said in the introduction of this book, the presidents who visited Maine reflected the times in which they served in office. The visit of President Trump came at a time when the state, the country, and the world was fighting the COVID-19 virus. The virus was the reason for the presidential visit—President Trump visited Puritan Medical Products in Guilford, a company on the front line fighting the virus, producing diagnostic supplies to help in the pandemic.

President Trump's visit was, as was his presidency, controversial. People criticized the timing of the visit and the rhetoric that proceeded it. The visit also coincided with the death of an African American citizen named George Floyd, who died after a police officer kneeled on his neck for a period of nine minutes. The incident, which sadly was not isolated, caused violent, deadly rioting in the streets of the country and different parts of the world, seeming to spread faster than the COVID-19 virus itself.

One of the things that is nice about the research and writing of history is that time has passed between the times of an event and the research of that event. Without the passage of time, history is just current events. Time has to pass, stories have to come out, words and actions have to be put in the perspective of time that has passed since the event.

With some of the Maine presidential visits, the man in the office was well-respected, sometimes not. While one may or may not agree with the person in office, the office of the president of the United States should always be respected, and not just by the citizens of our country, but also by the chosen few who occupy that office.

Sources

Bangor Daily Commercial
Bangor Daily News
Bangor Whig and Courier
Bar Harbor Record
Bar Harbor Tourist
Bar Harbor Times
Bath Daily Times
Becoming Teddy Roosevelt by Andrew Vietze, Copyright 2010, Down East Books
Boston Journal
Daily Kennebec Journal
Ellsworth American
Homefront on Penobscot Bay: Rockland during the War Years by Paul G. Merriam, Thomas J. Molloy, and Theodore W. Sylvester, Jr., Copyright 1991, Rockland Cooperative History Project
Lewiston Evening Journal
Mainers on the Titanic by Mac Smith, Copyright 2014, Down East Books
New York Times
New York Tribune
Portland Advertiser
Portland Evening Express
Portland Press Herald
The Republican Journal
The Washington Star

CPSIA information can be obtained
at www.ICGtesting.com
Printed in the USA
BVHW041524040921
615737BV00005B/12

9 781684 750122